roses

JimHole LoisHole

questions/ANSWERS

volume 2

roses

Practical Advice and the
Science Behind It

H
HOLE's
Enjoy Gardening

PUBLISHED BY HOLE'S
    101 Bellerose Drive
    St. Albert, Alberta Canada
    T8N 8N8

Copyright © 2000 Lois Hole

Printed in Canada   5   4   3   2   1

Canadian Cataloguing in Publication Data
Hole, Lois, 1933-
  Roses

  (Questions & answers ; 3)
  Includes index.
  ISBN 0-9682791-6-3

  1. Roses. 2. Rose culture. I. Hole, Jim, 1956- II. Title. III.
Series: Questions & answers (St. Albert, Alta.) ; 2.
SB411.5.C3H653 2000   635.9'33734   C00-910314-7

Printed and bound by Friesens, Altona, Manitoba, Canada.

Contents

Acknowledgements

For their years of dedicated help and their unsurpassed knowledge of roses, thanks to Shane Neufeld and Stephen Raven.

We also wish to thank the rest of our staff members, who carefully collected rose questions and supplied many of the answers.

Finally, thanks to all of you rosarians, who showed how much you love roses with the quality of your questions. You helped us learn much about these beautiful plants.

The Q&A Series— Practical Advice and the Science Behind It

Roses: Practical Advice and the Science Behind It is the second book in our new Q&A series. Why roses? Simply put, because we've received plenty of questions on the subject, and because we too love roses. We were thrilled to discover that gardeners' curiosity about roses is as boundless as the beauty of the blooms.

Success is built on a solid foundation of questions. Every innovation comes about because someone asked, "how does this process work? And how can I make it work better?" A good question can open up whole new worlds—new ways of doing things, new perspectives, and new information about secrets once hidden.

That information is what good gardening is all about. Our goal has always been to provide gardeners, no matter what their skill level, with the information they need to grow beautiful plants—and to accomplish this in the most enjoyable manner. Accordingly, different people want different kinds of information. We've answered the questions in two parts: a short answer for those who are eager to solve a problem and get back to their projects, and a more in-depth answer for those who want to spend a little time to learn what makes their favourite hobby tick. In short, we deliver practical advice and the science behind it.

At Hole's, we've always tried to ask the right questions, and to listen carefully when others ask questions of us. The questions in the Q&A books didn't spring from our heads—they were collected from hundreds of people, from coast to coast. Over the past dozen years, we've been recording the best questions we've run across, from the simple questions we thought beginning gardeners could identify with to the head-scratchers that gave us pause. The inquiries came from walk-in customers, letters, phone calls, and e-mails. Some came from audiences during one or another of our radio or television appearances; others from the folks we've spoken to at gardening talks all across the continent. A few came from our own employees during the day-to-day operations of our greenhouse. No matter what the source, each inquiry contained within itself a valuable piece of information: it told us what people wanted to know, and gave us a guide with which to build this series of books.

In seeking answers for these questions, we've learned a lot ourselves. The questioners have pushed us to the limits of our knowledge, urging us to dig deeper for the truth.

Lois Hole and Jim Hole

May 2000

Introduction

by Lois Hole

Roses have a magical presence—one that entices but also intimidates many gardeners. The truth is, growing great roses is no different than growing great vegetables, perennials, or bedding plants. All that is required is a willingness to ask the right questions and to challenge the myths. My son Jim and I, along with the rest of our family and staff, have spent years with these alluring plants, discovering their myriad secrets.

Roses on Arrival

Shortly after we were married, Ted and I took up residence on our new farm, just on the outskirts of St. Albert. In the beginning, the place was a little underdeveloped—in fact, practically the only thing left standing was a huge rosebush that looked just like the ones my Mom grew in my Saskatchewan hometown, Buchanan. The rose was growing next to the front door of the ramshackle little farmhouse, neglected but unbowed. For years, it produced big, deep-pink blooms and an enchanting fragrance that reminded me of Buchanan; I took to wearing the flowers in my hair during the summer. That rose, which I later discovered was of the Hansa variety, was a bright spot of beauty for many years, requiring very little effort to maintain. It has always been proof that roses can be very easy to grow.

A Thorny Gamble

Years later, after enjoying success with market gardening and wholesale vegetable production, we started our greenhouse business. We first started selling roses commercially back in 1982. The roses were almost an afterthought, coming as a part of a trees and shrubs package deal from one of our supply companies. We started with packaged roses, shipped in bags or boxes. But the roses looked rather anemic when we unpacked them. Bagged or boxed roses are easy to store and ship, but they're often small, lower-grade roses cut down even further to fit their packaging. Such roses are handicapped before you even plant them in the garden. Not surprisingly, many of these roses were returned to us by disappointed gardeners. We had quite a few guarantees to honour! (I should point out that not all bagged roses are bad—it all depends on the supplier and how the roses are handled at the point of sale.)

Hoping to improve customer satisfaction and reduce returns, we asked a different supplier to ship us some potted roses. We knew that potted roses cost more to grow, and are therefore more expensive for retailers and consumers alike, but we wanted to see what our customers valued more—a low price or a better plant. With limited experience, it was a bit of a gamble.

The First Shipment

The new arrivals came on our nursery manager Shane Neufeld's second day of work, and poor Shane sure had a mess to deal with. Not only were the 2500 roses loaded into the delivery truck in no particular order, many lacked even foliage! It looked as if the canes were just stuck into the pots, without any time to grow and establish themselves. Also, these roses were all of smaller, lower grades. To be sure, these potted roses were of better quality than the bagged and boxed roses we'd tried earlier, but there had to be room for improvement.

Going to Pot

Because of the rocky start and our desire to provide the best plants we possibly could, we decided to experiment a bit. To that end, Shane ordered a few bare-root roses. When they arrived in early spring, the roots didn't look terribly impressive: each was just a tangled knot of woody growth. But when we potted and grew them in our own greenhouses, they began to leaf out more vigorously than any roses we had had before. It took a number of

---

The Rose Experts

Shane Neufeld

Over the years, our rose-growing knowledge has increased tremendously thanks to the help of our two most trusted rose experts: Shane Neufeld and Stephen Raven.

Shane is our nursery manager and an ardent rose lover—though he didn't start out that way. "Truthfully, before we started growing roses here, I didn't really give them a second thought." Shane learned how to raise roses on the fly, experimenting in our greenhouses and picking up tips from his suppliers. "After working with roses for a few years, they've really grown on me—especially the hardy varieties like J.P. Connell and the other Explorer roses, all developed right here in Canada." Shane's willingness to experiment and his dedication to quality plants has been crucial to our growing understanding of roses.

Stephen is the head of our Shop by Mail department, and he's been growing roses for many years. The backyard of his St. Albert home is so full of roses that during the summertime the fragrance wafts through the whole neighbourhood...and the visual spectacle is even more enthralling. Stephen has over 150 varieties of roses, covering every rose category. "I have limited space," he says with a grin, "so I want to have as much diversity as possible." Stephen's love of roses and his years of experience in raising dozens of different varieties, especially the tender ones, have been invaluable.

Stephen Raven

different methods to achieve this. First, we built two cold frames just for roses so we could create an environment suited to their specific needs. Then Jim stepped in with some ideas. First, he suggested we replace the sawdust we used to supplement the soilless mix in the pots with a rich bark mix. That resulted in rich bloom colour. Jim then got the idea to put our roses on the same fertilization regimen we used on our bedding plants, switching from the typical slow-release granular fertilizer to the quick-release liquid feed our annuals enjoyed. The switch worked wonderfully, improving leafy growth, root development, and blooming of our roses.

But then we faced a business choice. There was no disputing that the roses were top-notch, but there's a cost associated with raising roses under such carefully controlled conditions. Would customers shell out the extra dollars for quality, or would they balk at the price?

Well, we've been potting our own roses for many years now, and we've found that people want quality. When we first starting selling roses, we only carried about 1,500 per year. These days, we sell over 10,000 roses each season. To me, that says that people put a premium on excellent plants.

Every year we learn a little more and continue to improve our growing methods. Just last year, we built a retractable-roof greenhouse over our nursery, in large part because we wanted to start more of our roses earlier in the season. As a result, we enjoy blooming roses in early April. And this year, we grew 100 potted roses in our main growing range, using bottom heat and larger pots to create truly massive rosebushes before Mother's Day.

A Change in Perception

Many gardeners perceive all roses as delicate, sensitive plants, and that's just not the case. Sure, many are tender and could die over the winter if not properly prepared for the season. But why not look at tender roses like annuals? For $20, you can get a lovely tender rosebush that will produce dozens of blooms during the summer—try to get the equivalent number of cut-roses for that price!

If that thought holds no appeal, there are dozens of beautiful hardy varieties available, with more appearing each year. Many, like the Explorer and Parkland roses, were developed right here in Canada.

There's no reason to be afraid of growing roses. Whatever your level of experience, there's a rose out there that's just perfect for your garden.

The Structure of Rose Gardening

Although we got into professional rose growing at the same time, Jim and I each look at rose gardening in a different way. I tend to appreciate the simple things—the fragrance of a rose, its silky texture, the simple fun of planting a rosebush. Jim, on the other hand, has an overriding curiosity about why roses grow the way they do. Unlike most gardeners, his first reaction upon seeing a bug or disease of some kind infesting his plants isn't horror—it's curiosity. To be sure, he's no fan of aphids and blackspot, but before he rushes for some means of eradication, Jim likes to think about why pests or disease appeared in the first place. Jim searches for causes, rather than simply reacting to effects.

Of course, there's some overlap in our attitude: I'm certainly curious about the science behind roses, and Jim isn't immune to their intrinsic beauty. But by and large, our answers to your rose questions tend to follow the pattern I describe.

This book is divided into seven sections that follow the progress of a typical season of rose gardening.

The Basics

Whether you're a newcomer to roses or an experienced rosarian, it never hurts to take a close look at the basics. A true understanding of the differences between species, cultivars, growth habits, and the "official" rose categories is a vital tool in rose gardening.

Choosing Roses

A rose by any other name would smell as sweet...on the other hand, if you buy a Cupcake or Morden Ruby expecting fragrance, you'll be in for a surprise. Choosing the right variety for your needs is an art, but one that you'll excel in given some simple guidelines.

Starting

Enjoying success with roses hinges upon the first steps you take in the garden. Planting a rose is really quite simple, but there are a few tricks that can get roses off to a better start. Just knowing the proper depth to plant roses is a good place to begin.

Growing

Here's where the magic happens. Nurturing a rose to its peak potential is one of the biggest rewards in the garden, and all it takes is the proper application of sound growing principles. When we started to pot roses, we followed the old growers' adage, "prune before you pot," snipping off large bits of the bare-root plants before sticking them in the pots. But after a while, we started to question why we were hacking off perfectly good growth. Once we turned the saying around to "pot before you prune," our roses grew much better. It only makes sense—why set back a rose before it even gets into the pot?

Enjoy Roses

Roses put on one of nature's most spectacular shows, but their beauty and usefulness isn't limited to the garden. You may not know, for example, that rose petals and rosehips are edible. My mother and aunt, twin sisters, ate rosehips by the handful all the years that they grew roses. I'm not saying there's a firm connection between rosehips and longevity, but my mother is still going strong at 94 years of age, and my aunt lived to 93. I will say, though, that all of the vitamin C in those rosehips probably contributed to their health!

Troubleshooting

Even during the best season, a problem or two is sure to crop up. I recall one lady who came in and claimed that a rosebush she'd purchased from us had brought powdery mildew into her garden. It turns out that the "mildew" on the rosebush was merely some harmless residue from a fungicide treatment we'd given the rose prior to sale. Even so, she was right to keep a close eye on her plants—careful observation helps catch problems early on, when they're much easier to rectify.

Varieties

Each rose variety has its own particular characteristics, its strengths and weaknesses. Match your expectations to the strengths of a rose, and you'll never be disappointed by its performance. On the other hand, allow yourself the joys of experimentation. With over one hundred species and many more varieties, there's a rose out there for each individual taste.

The Name of the Rose Game

A rose garden can be as simple as a single bush in a quiet corner of the yard, or a massive display that rivals the pageantry of a royal wedding. Both are legitimate expressions of the beauty and potential of roses, but the size of the display isn't the most important thing. To me, rose gardening is all about taking pleasure in the challenge of growing roses, enjoying their beauty, and having some fun along the way.

CHAPTER 1 ❦
THE BASICS

Great roses begin with the basics. A gorgeous show of blooms depends upon your knowledge of the fundamentals: the difference between types of roses, what constitutes good soil, the effect of climate, and more.

It's taken a long time for rose characteristics to be established. Fossil evidence found in Colorado and Oregon reveals that the plant genus Rosa is more than 30 million years old. People first began cultivating roses in North Africa 4,000 to 5,000 years ago. Today, there are at least 100 botanical species in the genus Rosa, and approximately 20,000 different varieties of rose. Sound complicated? Not at all. As long as you have a firm grasp of the basics, you'll be able to grow any of those varieties.

I've always been a little afraid to try growing roses. Is it as tricky as I think it is?

Lois ❖ It can be quite simple, if you want it to be. The hardy, rugged varieties are as reliable and easy to care for as any plant you could put in your garden. If you're growing roses for the first time, they provide a great place to start.

Jim ❖ When people tell me they're afraid to try growing a particular plant, it usually means they're afraid they'll kill it. However, there's no reason to worry, especially with hardy roses.

Tender roses do require more attention than hardy roses, but you shouldn't be afraid to try them. The main "trick" to growing tender roses is simply to take the time to look after them properly.

I've never grown roses before, but I'd like to. Where should I start?

Jim ❖ You're off to a good start. It's always a good idea to get your hands on a reliable reference book before trying something new in your garden.

I also tell first-time rose gardeners to start out with at least two bushes— one hardy and one tender. That way you're likely to have success on your first try and you'll learn first-hand which kind suits you best.

What does cultivar mean? What's the difference between a cultivar and a species?

Lois ❖ Cultivar is a shortened form of "cultivated variety." In plain language, this means that the plant variety exists because of human intervention. A rose growing out in the wild is not a cultivar, it is a species rose.

Jim ❖ Cultivar is one of those fancy words that people throw around, often not knowing exactly what it means. Mom's right—strictly speaking, some rose varieties can't truly be called cultivars. When it comes to roses, however, the terms "cultivar" and "variety" have become interchangeable.

A species is a population of organisms that can interbreed freely with one another but does not, because of geographic, reproductive or other barriers, interbreed with organisms outside the group.

Often, several rose species can be cross-bred to create a single rose variety.

Categories

What's the difference between a tender rose and a hardy rose?

Lois ❖ Tender roses need extra protection to survive year after year in areas with harsh winters. Hardy roses, on the other hand, overwinter without any extra protection.

Jim ❖ Some rose species have adapted over time to withstand cold winter temperatures. Breeders have been able to incorporate this hardiness into a wide (and widening) range of hybrids. The Parkland and Explorer series are among the most outstanding achievements of Canadian plant breeders.

Tender roses need extra protection to get through the winter—e.g., Floribunda, Hybrid Tea, Grandiflora, English and some Old Garden. Most tender roses were derived from varieties that originated in southern China (*Rosa chinensis*), which are not adapted to cold winters. Hardy roses—e.g., Parkland and Explorer Roses—need no extra winter protection. Treat them like any other shrubs—prior to winter, just water them well and clean up any dead leaves.

What is an old garden rose?

Lois ❖ For me, the term conjures up visions of the rose gardens I knew when I was growing up. The bushes were large and well established, and covered with fragrant pink roses. Most of the old garden rose varieties are pink.

Jim ❖ An old garden rose is a term of classification used for roses such as the moss, musk, and damask rose. It refers to varieties that have been cultivated since before 1867, when the first modern roses were introduced. Old garden roses generally have a limited but abundant blooming season, and produce full, fragrant flowers. In harsher climates, many old garden roses are considered borderline hardy.

What is a species rose?

Lois ❖ Any wild rose growing in its wild state is a species rose. The vast majority of rose varieties are hybrids.

Jim ❖ There are over 100 different species of roses throughout the world. In Alberta, the species rose we're most familiar with is the prickly rose (*Rosa acicularis*), our provincial floral emblem.

What is a hybrid rose? Is it the same as a hybrid tea?

Lois ❖ The vast majority of roses grown today are hybrids—that is to say they were produced by cross-pollinating different rose species. "Hybrid tea," on the other hand, refers specifically to one class of rose hybrids.

Jim ❖ If you go far enough back in time, all roses share a common ancestor. Gradually, though, roses in different areas of the world evolved into distinct species, each with its own genetic profile. When roses from two different species cross-pollinate, the result is a hybrid. Mom's right—most roses are hybrids. In fact, there are now approximately 20,000 hybrid varieties.

If you picture a classic, long-stemmed rose, it's a hybrid tea. They tend to grow long and lanky, but many hybrid teas produce spectacular, fragrant blossoms. When rosarians mark a dividing line between old and modern roses, they usually place it at 1867, the year the first hybrid tea rose ("La France") was introduced in Lyons, France.

Some roses are called "remontant". What does this mean?

Lois ❖ Every hobby has its own jargon! Roses described as "remontant" bloom more than once each season.

Jim ❖ "Remontant" actually means the rose blooms, stops, blooms, stops, etc. This is often mistakenly called "repeat blooming." "Repeat blooming" roses are those that bloom continuously. In French, "remontant" means "coming up again."

Morden Blush—double flower, hardy shrub

Main Official Rose Categories

Jim ❖ In this section we tackle a complicated and often controversial topic: how to divide roses into clear, official categories. The genus *Rosa* includes over 100 different species and over 20,000 different varieties. The "official" rose categories tend to be based on arbitrary decisions, rather than on growth habit or appearance. At the same time, there are endless regional variations in the way some terms are used. For instance, in this book when we use the term "shrub rose," we're referring only to hardy shrubs—not tender shrubs like the floribundas.

In any case, the following pages list the most widely accepted, "official" rose categories.

Categorizing roses is a controversial topic. There are official categories, but they tend to be arbitrary. At Hole's we tend to classify tender shrub roses as floribunda and reserve the shrub category for the hardy shrub roses. Climbers are a distinct group, but there are ramblers, trailing and groundcover roses, too, and there also are Explorers (hardy shrub) which can be trained to climb. In this book we will refer to hardy shrub roses as a separate category

Their wide geographic distribution combined with extensive hybridization has made roses difficult to classify. The official categories are often based on arbitrary decisions rather than the look or growth habit of a rose.

Hybrid tea
- Upright remontant shrubs
- Flowers bloom singly or in very small clusters (two to three)
- A few single, but mostly double flowers
- Large flowers, usually fragrant
- Blooms from summer right through to fall
- Originated as a cross between Tea Rose and Hybrid Perpetual, in 1867

Floribunda
- Upright remontant shrubs
- Single or double flowers in clusters of 3 to 25
- Blooms summer through fall
- First Floribundas were "Else Poulsen" and "Kirsten Poulsen" in 1924, although the class wasn't recognized and given the name Floribunda until the 1950s

Grandiflora
- An intermediate between Floribunda and Hybrid Tea
- Usually double flowers
- Upright remontant shrubs
- Smaller clusters than Floribunda, but larger flowers
- Smaller flowers than Hybrid Tea, but generally taller bushes
- Bloom summer through fall

Miniature
- Upright remontant shrubs
- Height varies from 15-60 cm
- Single to double flowers in clusters
- Looks like smaller versions of hybrid teas

English
- Most are remontant shrubs
- Most have double flowers
- Noted for old-fashioned look and heavy fragrance
- New class of roses created by David Austin; a result of crosses between modern and Old Garden roses

Polyantha
- Compact remontant shrubs
- Single flowers
- Many small flowers in clusters
- Blooms summer to fall
- Originally a mixed group, derived from *Rosa moschata*, *Rosa chinensis* and *Rosa multiflora*; by the early 1900s, Polyanthus had developed into a fairly uniform group

Old Garden Rose
- Very diverse group, comprising lots of different types and cultivars
- Some single but usually double flowers
- Term is used to describe the roses (none of them species roses) grown by people up until the advent of Hybrid Teas in 1867
- Includes Tea Rose, Alba, Bourbon, Centifolia, Chinensis, Damascena, Gallica, Moss, Hybrid Musk and Hybrid Perpetual

Shrub
- A description rather than a specific bloodline—used as a catch-all name for roses that don't fit in other categories
- Single or double flowers
- Generally grows taller than 1 metre when mature
- Can flower once, repeatedly, or continuously, depending on the variety
- Includes Hardy Shrub Roses

Species Rose
- Any of the wild roses, found in their natural state
- Usually single flowers
- Widely diverse range of plants
- Usually only bloom once per season

Climbers
- Long, stiff shoots
- Single or double flowers
- Bears single blooms or clusters
- Can flower once, repeatedly, or continuously, depending on the variety
- Parentage of this distinct group can include Hybrid Teas and Floribundas

Tender and Hardy Roses

Hardy and Tender Roses are classifications based solely on whether or not the plants will survive harsh winters. As we all have our own definition of "harsh," this classification also has significant variation.

Tender
Hybrid Tea
Floribunda
Grandiflora
Miniature
Landscape
English
Polyantha
Old Garden Rose
Tea Roses
Bourbon
Centifolias
Chinensis
Damascena
Moss
Hybrid Musk
Hybrid Perpetual
Tender Shrub
Species Rose (various)
Climbing (various)

Hardy
Hardy Shrub
Parkland
Pavement
Explorer
Old Garden Rose
Alba
Some Bourbon
Centifolias
Some Damascena
Gallica
Species Rose
Rugosa
Most Hybrid Spinossima
Climbing (various)

Paradise—double flower, hybrid tea

Rose Classification

For decades, rosarians have struggled to create a single, standardized system for rose classification. The terms we use now are vague and overlap endlessly. If two rosarians try to classify a particular specimen, chances are their descriptions won't match. With over 20,000 cultivars, and hundreds of new ones being added each year, the challenge is becoming more and more difficult.

At the first World Rose Convention in 1971, delegates approved a new classification system. They decided to divide roses according to growth habit—climbing (I) vs. non-climbing (II)—and flowering habit—recurrent (A) vs. nonrecurrent (B). In this system, for example, a rose that climbs and flowers recurrently would be classed as I-A. Unfortunately, rosarians on the whole still haven't fully embraced this system.

Grower's edge

One year a customer complained to me that her hybrid tea rose died over the winter. She said she never would have bought it if she had known it was hard to overwinter. I asked her how many flowers she got from it before it died. "At least 50 beautiful flowers," she replied. Well then, don't get upset, I told her—to get that many roses at a flowershop would have cost over $100—an excellent value!

General characteristics

How do I know if roses will grow in my climate?

Lois ❖ Don't worry—all roses will grow. What you really want to know is if a rose will survive the winter! You may want to stick to hardy roses, if you don't want to do the extra work involved in growing tender roses. Keep in mind, though, that most tender roses produce dozens of blooms each year. They're worth the price, even if they only survive for one growing season. Do your best to protect them through the winter, but be philosophical if they don't always come back!

Jim ❖ One thing I've learned in all these years of gardening is to never say that a plant won't grow in one region or another. No sooner do I say it than sure as heck some gardener will say, "Well, I've been growing it for years." The key to growing roses in our climate is winter protection. The more tender the rose, the more winter protection it requires. Many yards have microclimates near heated foundations or fences that make growing tender varieties possible.

Talk to the rose experts at your garden centre or do some research on your own to determine which flowers you need to protect.

How much sun do roses need?

Lois ❖ As much sun as you can give them! The more sunlight they receive, the better they grow and the more they bloom. The only time that shade can be beneficial is on very hot days in the afternoon. I never plant a rose in a spot that doesn't get at least 6 hours of direct sunlight per day.

Keep in mind that the sunlight is less intense during the evening and early morning. You want your roses to get at least some sun during the day's brightest hours, from late morning to late afternoon.

Jim ❖ Six hours or more is best, but most roses can grow quite well with as little as four hours of direct sunlight per day. Just keep in mind that as you reduce the amount of sunlight, you can expect a corresponding decrease in foliage and flowers. In the greenhouse in February and March, we provide supplemental light to increase flower numbers and shorten the time to bloom. We use 400-watt high-intensity discharge lights (HIDs) from 5 pm until 9 am. The roses get 24 hours of light.

However, in some regions with intense, hot summers, a bit of afternoon shading will help your roses produce bigger flowers and better colour. Blooms that receive too much hot sunlight age quickly and are very pale. Those plants also consume extra water.

Will roses grow under spruce trees?

Lois ❖ Spruce trees compete with any plant for light, space, and moisture. The closer you plant your rose to the spruce, the more difficulty you'll have growing it.

Jim ❖ It's hard enough to get grass to grow under a spruce, never mind roses. Don't put your rose any closer than your tree's longest horizontal branches. Even so, you'll have to water and fertilize much more often. I just don't recommend planting near a spruce tree.

How long will it take for my rose to reach its full size?

Lois ❖ It all depends on the variety. Many container-grown roses put on a marvellous display within weeks of being transplanted, while others (such as shrub roses) take several years to come into their own.

Jim ❖ Climbing roses continue to grow and spread, and theoretically never reach their mature height. Hybrid tea, Floribunda, Grandiflora, and Polyanthus all reach mature height in the first year, provided they get a good start.

Can roses survive frosts?

Lois ❖ Definitely. I've seen fully leafed, flowering roses of all types survive a bout of spring frost. Roses are tougher than you might think!

Jim ❖ We've noted that fully leafed-out roses can survive down to at least -9°C with only minimal damage to the new shoots, provided we acclimatize them gradually to handle cooler temperatures.

When you're talking about over the winter, however, a rose's cold tolerance depends largely on the variety, and how well it's been hardened off during the fall. Another factor is how much protection or snow cover it has. Most yards have several microclimates that can afford roses more protection from cold.

Apart from winterkill, how delicate are roses? If I occasionally forget to water or fertilize, will my roses die?

Lois ❖ They might if you're growing them in containers. Since they can't draw any moisture or nutrients from the soil outside the pot, they rely completely on you.

If you neglect the roses in your garden, they won't die, but they'll flower poorly. Once you start giving them the water and fertilizer they need, you won't believe the difference. Neglect results in weaker plants that are more susceptible to disease and infestations. If you do have a tendency to forget, stick with species and hardy shrub roses. They're the most forgiving.

Jim ❖ Tender roses aren't difficult to grow, but they need regular care. Hybrid Tea, Grandiflora and Floribunda in particular all need a good, steady supply of water and fertilizer to perform at their best. If you neglect them, you'll notice that they're not producing many flowers. Give them the attention they crave (regular water and fertilizer), however, and they'll really put on a show for you. They're well worth the extra effort.

Soil

What kind of soil do roses prefer?

Lois ❖ Roses like soil that's rich in organic matter—a deep loamy soil is best.

Why is my soil's pH important?

Jim ❖ First let's review our chemistry. The pH scale represents the alkalinity of a solution. On this scale, 7.0 is exactly neutral–neither acidic nor alkaline. As the numbers decrease (6.9, 6.8 etc.), the acidity increases. As the numbers rise (7.1, 7.2 etc.), the alkalinity increases.

In alkaline soil, chemical compounds tend to be less soluble. This means that there are fewer nutrients available to your plants.

Like most perennial plants, roses perform best in slightly acidic soil (6.2–6.5). However, if the soil is too acidic (lower than 6.2), plants absorb excessive quantities of some nutrients, resulting in toxic levels. As well, many beneficial soil microorganisms cannot survive in very acidic soils.

Roses prefer a rich, slightly acidic soil with a pH of 6.2–6.5. However, I have seen roses do very well in extremely acidic soil (down to pH 5.0). The only way to determine if your soil falls within this range is with a soil test. Here in Alberta, soils range from the very alkaline (high pH) in the southeast regions to the acidic in the boggy, boreal forest regions of the north. As a rule, high pH is a much more common problem than low pH.

Once you do a soil test to determine the pH, you can adjust your soil accordingly to reach the ideal level.

How do I adjust my soil's pH?

Lois ❖ Assuming you have had your soil tested, take the results to a good garden centre. A staff member should be able to give you reliable advice on how to deal with your soil's pH.

Jim ❖ To adjust pH, you have to amend your soil. Sulphur and sulphur–containing compounds lower the pH (making your soil more acidic), while dolomite (lime) raises the pH. You can purchase these compounds at most garden centres.

If you're adding sulphur, stick with fine sulphur or iron sulphate—coarse sulphur reacts very slowly.

The amount of sulphur or lime you add to your soil depends to a large extent on the type of soil you have. Here is a rough guideline.

How much sulphur/lime to add to soil to change pH levels

GARDEN SULPHUR* 0.5 kg/100 m^2 (acidifier—to lower pH)

Desired pH Change	Sands	Loam	Clay
8.5 6.5	46	57	68
8.0–6.5	27	34	46
7.5–6.5	11	18	23
7.0–6.5	2	3	6

* although sulphur is effective, it is slow to react to soil

LIMESTONE 0.5 kg/100 m^2 (basifier—to increase pH)

Desired pH Change	Sandy loam	Loam	Silt Loam	Clay
4.0–6.5	115	160	193	230
4.5–6.5	96	133	193	230
5.0–6.5	78	105	128	151
5.5 6.5	60	78	91	105
6.0–6.5	32	41	50	55

Should I add lime to my soil?

Jim ❖ If your soil has only a slightly acidic pH (between 6.2-6.5), lime will do more harm than good! Only add it if a soil test indicates that your soil is too acidic.

Here are a few quick facts on horticultural lime (dolomite).

- Its main effect on soil is to raise the pH. When a soil is too acidic, your plants absorb toxic amounts of some nutrients. Adding lime raises the pH, and balances your plants' uptake of nutrients. If you add lime to soil that doesn't need it, however, you risk making your soil too alkaline. When that happens, your plants can't absorb enough of the nutrients they need.

- Many beneficial soil microorganisms (those that break down organic matter) cannot survive in very acidic soils.

- Lime adds nutrients to the soil (in the case of dolomite, CaMg). However, most soils already contain enough calcium and magnesium to sustain healthy plant growth.

Should I add manure to the soil?

Lois ❖ Yes! Roses just love rich soil. Make sure to use only well-rotted manure in order to avoid burning your plants.

Jim ❖ Manure and compost provide nutrients, improve soil texture, and help soil retain moisture. All the plants in your garden grow better if you add manure and compost regularly. Roses in particular thrive in soils enriched with well-composted manure.

Typical Composition of Manures

Source	Dry Matter (%)	Approximate Composition (% dry weight)		
		N	P_2O_5	K_2O
Dairy	15–25	0.6–2.1	0.7–1.1	2.4–3.6
Feedlot	20–40	1.0–2.5	0.9–1.6	2.4–3.6
Horse	15–25	1.7–3.0	0.7–1.2	1.2–2.2
Poultry	20–30	2.0–4.5	4.5–6.0	1.2–2.4
Sheep	25–35	3.0–4.0	1.2–1.6	3.0–4.0
Swine	20–30	3.0–4.0	0.4–0.6	0.5–1.0

What are epsom salts? Are they good for roses?

Jim ❖ The chemical name for epsom salts is magnesium sulphate, $Mg(SO_4)_2$. Epsom salts contain magnesium and sulphur, two essential nutrients for rose growth and health. In the greenhouse, we test our soil and add epsom salts if necessary. However, most garden soils contain adequate amounts of magnesium and sulphur, so epsom salts normally don't provide any real benefit.

Magnesium deficiency in roses shows up on lower leaves first, giving them a veiny look (iron causes a veiny look on new growth). Sulphur deficiency is rare, but turns the entire plant yellow-green (much like nitrogen deficiency).

Epsom salts can be good for roses, but soil scientists have a phrase that is sound advice if you're planning to supplement your soil—"Don't guess, soil test!"

How deep should the topsoil be in my rose bed?

Lois ❖ The deeper the topsoil, the better, but you should start with at least 30 cm. My daughter-in-law Valerie has 50 cm of topsoil in all her rose beds.

Jim ❖ Good, deep topsoil allows for better root development. Roses with deep and vigorous roots are more drought tolerant during the summer, and better equipped to survive through the winter.

My garden has heavy clay soil.
What should I do if I want to grow roses in it?

Lois ❖ The good news is that roses prefer clay-based soil. If your soil is particularly heavy, though, work in plenty of organic material—well-rotted manure, compost, and peat moss. You may also want to top dress your beds with good black loam.

Jim ❖ As Mom mentioned, organic matter is excellent for loosening clay soil. It binds the clay into clumps, allowing air and water to penetrate the soil more easily. Well-rotted manure, compost, and peat moss loosen the soil, and improve its drainage, aeration and its ability to retain moisture. Gypsum (a type of lime)—$Ca(SO_4)_2$—has much the same effect on clay soils, but it's no substitute for adding organic matter because it doesn't contain any nutrients.

Improving heavy soil takes some commitment and effort. You may have to work at it for a few seasons. However, you'll reap the benefits for many years to come.

What roses grow well in poor soil?

Lois ❖ Species roses and hardy shrubs are your best bets, but no rose performs up to its potential in substandard soil. Instead of looking for a variety that tolerates poor soil, simply take steps to improve the soil. The roses will be happier and so will you!

Jim ❖ No matter what the variety, I promise you that a rose will do much better in good soil than it will in poor soil. You'll get bigger, more abundant flowers, and more attractive foliage. There's little satisfaction in growing a stunted rose! Unless you're willing to provide your roses with rich, fertile soil, you might as well not plant them at all.

Some Species Roses

Red Rugosa
Red-leaf Rose
Sweetbriar Rose
White Rugosa
Wingthorn Rose

I'm growing hybrid tea roses in pots. What kind of soil should I use?

Lois ❖ We use a special mix for all our roses, but any good-quality potting soil will do very nicely. Don't use regular garden soil for your potted roses, or for any other plants grown in containers. Garden soil contains weeds and easily becomes compacted.

Jim ❖ Potting soil provides good drainage, water retention, nutrients, and the proper pH. And unlike garden soil, potting soil is free of weeds and pests, and doesn't become hard and compacted. Five years ago, we started growing all our containers roses in a high-quality bark-peat moss mix and saw immediate improvement in leaf colour and size and bud count. It proved to be one of the easiest and best "improvements" we could have made.

Red-leaf Rose—single flower, hardy species rose

CHAPTER 2 ❦
CHOOSING

*Before you purchase a rose, you should take
the time to establish your goals and your
growing conditions. What's your favourite
flower colour? If you live in a very cold
climate, are you willing to grow tender roses
as annual bedding plants, or would you
prefer a hardy variety that will last for years?*

*It's also crucial to take an inventory of
the characteristics of your favourite
rose varieties. You need to know if your
favourite climber, which thrived in
Vancouver, will grow to similar heights
in Thompson, Manitoba.*

*It doesn't matter which rose you choose,
as long as your choice is informed.
Enter your garden centre armed
with knowledge and your rose-growing
experience will be that much better.*

Why would I choose a tender rose over a hardier one? What makes it worth the extra work?

Lois ❖ As a rule, tender roses are much showier than hardy roses. They come in a wider range of colours, produce larger, more abundant blooms, and produce better cutflowers. Best of all, most of them have a much longer blooming period each growing season. If you are going to grow roses, I recommend you try at least one tender rose.

Jim ❖ In gardening, you have to accept the fact that the most rewarding plants often require a bit more effort. If you're looking for the kind of perfect, long-stemmed blooms you buy at a florist, you won't find them on many hardy roses. However, with the efforts of rose breeders, this is gradually changing.

Until then, remember that a tender rose can richly reward you for your investment, even if it only survives for one season. A single tender shrub may produce dozens of blooms. In fact, many of our customers treat tender roses as annuals. I encourage you, however, to try to protect them over the winter. It's not that much work, and you'll be surprised at how many of your roses survive to bloom again next year.

What's a zone?

Lois ❖ Zones are areas that have similar winter temperatures. The higher the zone number (from 0 to 10), the milder the winter. Like other perennial plants, roses are often rated for their hardiness using these zone numbers.

Jim ❖ Zones are ranked from 0 to 10, based largely on a region's coldest winter temperatures. Zone 0 has permafrost, while zone 10 never freezes. Northern ranges of Alberta, Saskatchewan, Manitoba, Quebec, and B.C. all have zone 1 conditions, while the mid-ranges of these provinces are zone 2–4. Canada has no zone 10 regions, but some small coastal areas in B.C. boast zone 9a conditions. (The zones are broken down into sub zones a and b—b is about 5°C warmer in winter than its partner a.)

When checking hardiness, remember a rose rated hardy to zone 5 needs extra winter protection in zones 4 and below.

How do I know what zone I live in?

Lois ❖ Simply find your region on a zone map. You can find zone maps in books, garden centres, and even on the World Wide Web.

Jim ❖ The map gives the official zone designation. However, in practice, you often find several microclimates in a single area, or even in a single yard! For instance, a hybrid tea rose that would die out in a zone 2 garden might overwinter just fine if you plant it next to your house's foundation and give it a bit of winter protection.

For example, our area is zone 3a, but most plants rated zone 4 survive very well and we have had plants rated to zone 5 and even 6 survive our winters easily.

Which roses are hardy in areas that have harsh winters?

Lois ❖ North America encompasses a wide range of climates. Assuming you live in zone 2 or higher, many rose varieties will overwinter if given adequate protection.

Jim ❖ When it comes to winter hardiness, there are really only two categories of roses—those that need winter protection and those that don't.

No winter protection
• Explorers
• Parklands
• Hardy Shrub
• Most Species

Winter protection
• Hybrid Tea
• English
• Floribunda
• Grandiflora
• Miniature
• Old Garden Roses

Granada—double flower, hybrid tea, very fragrant

Altaica—single flower, hardy species rose

Will any roses survive in zone 1?

Lois ❖ I always admire the adventurous spirit of the zone 1 gardeners! They're willing to try growing almost anything, just to prove that they can conquer the climate. To be certain of success, however, I'd recommend sticking to the hardiest of the hardy roses and planting in a sheltered area which receives plenty of good snow cover.

Jim ❖ The tough Explorer roses, the Rugosa roses, and the wild rose all do quite well in zone 1 climates. If you want to test the limits by growing something more tender, you'll really have to give it extra protection over the winter. Thoughtful manipulation of the microclimates in your yard can go a long way to defeating the harshness of zone 1 winters.

I've learned not to predict what's possible in zone 1—I've been proven wrong too many times!

How do I know if a rose that is hardy somewhere else will survive in our climate?

Lois ❖ Despite all the "expert" opinion, there's really no way of knowing ahead of time whether or not a rose will survive in your yard. All you can do is try!

You can always ask at a local garden centre or horticultural club. And keep in mind that most tender roses put on a beautiful show in their first growing season. They're always worth the investment, even if some of them don't return the following spring.

Jim ❖ If you live in a northern climate, you know the importance of dressing for the weather! Just like people, most roses can make it through the winter if they have a few layers of extra protection. Some of the most tender roses are only hardy down to -5°C or so, and must be buried or heavily mulched to survive a winter.

One tip I always give to people trying to overwinter tender roses is to stop removing hips after the end of August. As the remaining hips ripen fully, the entire plant prepares itself for winter, making it much more resistant to winter injury.

F.J. Grootendorst—double flower, hardy shrub

Are there hardy roses that look like tender roses?

Lois ❖ Not quite, but breeders are getting closer all the time! Many hardy roses look very similar to their more tender cousins, producing spectacular clusters of blooms throughout the summer and fall. However, no hardy rose produces the kind of single, long-stemmed blooms you'll find on a hybrid tea.

Jim ❖ Try Champlain, Frontenac, George Vancouver, J.P. Connell, Morden Blush, Morden Fireglow, Morden Cardinette, Centennial, Winnipeg Parks, or Ruby. Hardy roses really have come a long way in the past few decades.

There are so many varieties of hardy roses, I can't decide which one to grow. What are the hardiest?

Lois ❖ The Explorer roses, the Parkland roses, and the Hansa Rose are all outstanding choices. I grew Hansa roses around my house for years with minimal effort.

Jim ❖ Remember that the hardiest rose won't necessarily give you the most satisfaction. Don't be afraid to experiment and find something that suits your tastes. With so many colours and scents to choose from, you shouldn't simply limit yourself to the hardiest roses.

George Vancouver—double flower, hardy shrub

Frontenac—double flower, hardy shrub

Where should I buy my roses?

Lois ❖ Shop at a good garden centre, where they know how to care for roses. The cheap, boxed plants you see at the grocery or department store may be tempting, but you're far better off spending your money on healthy, well-established container-grown roses.

Jim ❖ Find a garden centre with a wide selection of container-grown roses, and well-trained staff to offer you advice.

Always buy only top-quality roses, even if they cost a bit more.

What are rose grades?

Jim ❖ Roses come in three grades. Grade 1 roses have three or more stout, 45-cm canes. Grade 1½ have two 38-cm canes and Grade 2 have two 30-cm canes.

You can also buy ungraded roses, which are often marked as "two-year-old field grown." Grade these yourself by measuring the size of the stems.

What should I consider when buying a rose plant?

Lois ❖ As with any plant, the more mature the better. I recommend getting a Grade 1 plant. It will establish itself and mature much more quickly than a Grade 1½ or 2.

Choose a potted rose that's already in bud or flower. That way you can see the colour and shape of the blooms, and be sure that you're getting exactly the variety you want.

Jim ❖ If you're shopping for a hardy rose and you're patient, you might consider buying a Grade 2 rose. Personally, I'd rather pay the few extra dollars for a top-grade plant.

There are other advantages to buying mature plants. Large potted roses have been treated for mites, aphids and diseases prior to purchase. They have well-developed root systems (making them easier to transplant successfully) and have been pruned to produce many canes.

Is it better to buy a packaged or potted rose?

Lois ❖ Buy only potted roses! You'll be able to see exactly what you're buying, and you can be sure that it will produce lots of flowers the very first year.

Retailers often store and display boxed roses in areas that are too warm and too dimly lit. As a result, the plants begin to send out long, spindly shoots. Roses in this weakened state often don't survive transplanting.

Even worse, some packaged roses are dead when you buy them—but you don't find out about it until after they've been planted for several weeks.

Jim ❖ A container-grown rose is your best choice because:

• You can see exactly what you're buying.

• The plant has likely been treated at least once for insects and diseases.

• The growing medium in the pot contains fertilizer and other important amendments for your flowerbed.

• Large potted roses are often in bud and will bloom as soon as they're in your garden.

• A well-established plant has a much greater chance of surviving that all-important first winter.

If I decide to buy a packaged rose, how can I tell if it's healthy?

Lois ❖ You can't—all you can do is buy from a reputable supplier. The rose canes should be supple with small buds. Don't purchase a bush that has long, pale-white shoots of new growth. This means that the rose is in a weakened state and will take longer to grow. It is also more susceptible to insects and disease.

Jim ❖ Companies apply a waxy coating over the stems of dormant roses to protect them from drying out. Ironically, though, I've seen roses severely damaged from excessively hot wax—and unfortunately, you can't tell if that's a problem until you plant.

Also, check the weight of the package: a lightweight package likely means the soil around the plant is dry and needs watering—definitely not a good bet.

If you're buying a packaged rose, it's best to do so early in the season. A plant may be healthy when it arrives at the store, and then die on the shelf. Never buy a plant without taking a good close look at the wood. If the branches appear green and healthy, chances are the rose will survive. Keep in mind that packaged roses usually take two full years to become fully established. They may not produce many flowers in the first season, and (if you live in an area with harsh winters) they may not survive for a second season.

Why are some roses more fragrant than others?

Lois ❖ Sometimes when you stop and smell the roses, they'll disappoint you! Many varieties have little or no scent. Roses carry their scent largely in the petals. For instance, double roses are generally more fragrant than single roses.

In recent years, many rose breeders have devoted more of their efforts into developing particularly fragrant varieties.

Jim ❖ Some roses do get shortchanged in the scent department. Fragrance is a recessive trait, which means that when roses are bred, the non-fragrant characteristics predominate. Rose breeders love a challenge, however. They're proving that, with extra work, they can successfully breed roses for fragrance.

I've always wanted a rose hedge. Which varieties are best for this purpose?

Lois ❖ A well-tended rose hedge can be truly breathtaking! For a short hedge, use Pavement Roses or Double White Burnet. If you want a larger hedge, try Red or White Rugosa, or Scabrosa. Water and fertilize your hedge regularly, and you'll be the envy of the neighbourhood.

Jim ❖ Before investing in a formal chipped hedge, consider the work you'll have to do to keep it properly pruned. An informal hedge doesn't require any pruning, and produces more flowers.

Can I train my hardy shrub rose to climb?

Lois ❖ Yes, some cultivars work very well. Try a rose from the Explorer series such as John Davis or John Cabot.

Jim ❖ A climbing rose is just a sprawling rose that has been tied to or woven through a trellis or other support (roses don't have any tendrils that can wrap around trellises or posts). Any hardy rose with a sprawling habit and long flowering period makes a good candidate.

Some Fragrant Roses

Abraham Darby
Blanc Double de Coubert
Cabbage Rose
Double Delight
Evelyn
Fair Bianca
Fisherman's Friend
Fragrant Cloud
Gertrude Jekyll
Glamis Castle
Granada
Hansa
L.D. Braithwaite
Mme. Hardy
St. Swithun
Stanwell Perpetual
Tiffany

Gertrude Jekyll—double flower, English rose

Some Hedge Roses

Adelaide Hoodless
Blanc Double de Coubert
Champlain
Double White Burnet
F.J. Grootendorst
Fimbriata
Hansa
John Franklin
Marie Bugnet
Morden Fireglow
Pavement Roses
Red Rugosa
Red-leaf Rose
Scabrosa
The Hunter
White Rugosa
Winnipeg Parks

Champlain—double flower, hardy shrub

I'm hoping to grow some really huge, spectacular rose blooms. Which varieties produce the largest flowers?

Lois ❖ You can't go wrong with Royal Highness. It truly lives up to its name! This plant is a true show-stopper, producing dozens of gorgeous 15-cm flowers on long, elegant stems.

Jim ❖ You have hundreds of varieties to choose from! However, for size, some of my favourite choices would be St. Patrick, Peace, Electron, Elizabeth Taylor, Gertrude Jekyll, Gold Medal, Mister Lincoln, Olympiad, or Paradise.

I've got some big spaces to fill in my flowerbed. Can you recommend a really low-growing, wide-spreading rose?

Lois ❖ You'll be happy with Max Graf or Charles Albanel. Unlike many of the common hardy groundcover roses, these low-growing shrubs tend to bloom all season.

Jim ❖ The various Pavement Roses are all perfect for this. I've never met anyone who didn't like them. Nozomi is also particularly beautiful when it's in full bloom. It's not completely hardy, however, so you'll need to protect it in areas with harsh winters.

Are any rose varieties insect and disease resistant?

Jim ❖ If I had to suggest just one, I'd say to go with Rugosa. When plant breeders look for a species to help them create a hardy hybrid, they often turn to this amazingly sturdy plant. Best of all, it also produces lots of beautiful and usually fragrant blossoms.

I want to grow roses at our cabin at the lake, but I can't always be there to water them. Are there any varieties that are particularly drought-resistant?

Lois ❖ The Explorer and Morden series will tolerate a wide range of growing conditions. They won't bloom as much during a dry spell, but apart from that they'll be just fine. Remember, though, that any newly planted rose requires regular water for the first month or so until it is well established.

Jim ❖ You might want also want to consider planting wild roses. They've been around for thousands of years without anybody watering

Some Groundcover Roses

Charles Albanel
Dart's Dash
Double White Burnet
Frau Dagmar Hartopp
Max Graf
Nozomi
Pavement Roses
Red Frau Dagmar Hartopp

Some Explorer Roses

Alexander Mackenzie
Captain Samuel Holland
Champlain
Charles Albanel
David Thompson
Frontenac
George Vancouver
Henry Hudson
Henry Kelsey
J.P. Connell
Jens Munk
John Cabot
John Davis
John Franklin
Louis Jolliet
Martin Frobisher
Quadra
Simon Fraser
William Baffin

Jens Monk—double flower, hardy shrub

or fertilizing them. These have fragrant flowers, and most produce dazzling fall colour. If you're thinking of creating a more natural look in your garden, these are a great choice. They are available at some specialty garden centres.

Whatever varieties you plant, though, be sure to give them plenty of care each time you visit them at the lake.

I would like to plant an unusual or rare rose variety. Any suggestions?

Lois ❖ Without a doubt, the Wingthorn is the most unusual rose out there. Its large, brilliant red thorns are as showy as its blossoms! My husband Ted planted one beside our house several years ago, and it proved to be a real conversation piece.

Jim ❖ If you shop around, you'll find plenty of head-turning roses out there. My favourite is the Red-leaf rose. It has fine striking foliage that is almost dark purple and is Alberta bred. The Marie Bugnet, Louise Bugnet, and Rita Bugnet roses are difficult to find but are very hardy and are among the first roses to bloom in the spring.

What is a tree rose?

Lois ❖ A tree rose is simply a rosebush grafted onto the top of a long, single cane. Sometimes, the cane itself is also grafted at the bottom to rootstock. Tree roses make a truly striking addition to your rose bed.

Jim ❖ Tree roses are usually about 1–2 m tall. A few of the newer varieties are also hardy. If you live in an area with harsh winters, you must protect most tree roses over the winter. Dig the plants up in the fall, lay them on their sides in trenches, and completely bury them. Remember to mark the spot at both ends to prevent accidentally severing the cane and to ensure you can easily locate your tree rose next spring!

Unusual Roses

Wingthorn
Large, ruby-red thorns on tall, spiky stems

Scentimental
Red-and-white-striped flowers

Oranges and Lemons
Orange-and-yellow-striped flowers

Fimbriata
Blooms closely resemble soft pink carnations

F.J. Grootendorst
Red, carnation

Nigel Hawthorn
Scarlet-eyed flowers are bright, rosy salmon when they first open, and gradually fade to a soft salmon

Tigris
Yellow blossoms with bright-red eyes

Euphrates
Scarlet eyes contrasted against pale, salmon-pink petals

Ruffled Roses
Lovely peony-like flowers—not available until 2001

Do any rose varieties tolerate shade?

Lois ❖ "Tolerate" is the right word to use when you're talking about roses and shade. The rose varieties described as "shade tolerant" grow much more successfully in full sun. However, most roses will tolerate some shade for half the day. Keep in mind that your roses will not produce many blooms and those blooms will be smaller when your roses are planted in a shady location.

Some Shade-Tolerant Roses

Alain Blanchard
Alba Maxima
Alba Semi-plena
Botzaris
Cabbage Rose
Celestial
Charles de Mills
Double White Burnet
Frau Dagmar Hartopp
Frühlingsanfang
Frühlingsmorgen
Gruss an Aachen
Mme. Hardy
Nozomi
Red Frau Dagmar Hartopp
Rosa Mundi
Scabrosa
Schneezwerg
The Hunter
White Rugosa
Wingthorn Rose

Botzaris—double flower, old garden rose

CHAPTER 3 ❧
STARTING

*Like a beautiful butterfly emerging from
a grey cocoon, each rosebush has a
similarly humble beginning, whether it
comes from tiny seeds or gnarled bare roots.
If you get the first steps right, the rest of
the journey goes much more smoothly.*

*Take my father-in-law, for example.
He loved roses, and he tried to grow them all
his life—but no matter what poor Grandpa
Hole did, his rosebushes always seemed to
be straggly messes, with disappointing, short-
lived blooms. If only he'd taken the time to
learn where to plant them—Grandpa Hole
had an unfortunate tendency to place his
roses right in the shade of large trees.*

Seeding

Can I grow my own roses from seed?

Lois ❖ That chore is best left to breeders. Many seeds won't germinate. When two different species of roses cross-pollinate, they often produce sterile seed. Those seeds that grow often require at least two growing seasons to produce plants that are large enough to flower.

Jim ❖ If you want to try it go ahead; just be prepared for the occasional disappointment. Keep in mind, however:

- It takes much longer to grow a rose to maturity from seed than from cuttings.
- You must gather the seeds when the rose hips are full and ripe, but not wrinkled and soft. If you harvest the seeds too early or too late, they won't be viable.
- Rose seeds require stratification (long periods of cold, moist soil) before they will germinate.
- Seeds may be sterile—this is the case for many hybrids.
- The plants you produce may bear little resemblance to either parent plant.

Snow Pavement—double flower, hardy shrub

What special treatment do rose seeds require?

Jim ❖ Every rose seed has natural inhibitors in its seed coat, to prevent it from germinating until the following spring. Before rose seeds will germinate, you have to fool them into thinking they've experienced winter. We call this process "stratification." Store the seeds in a moist environment, at 2–4°C for periods ranging from six weeks to six months, depending on the variety.

Why are some seeds sterile?

Jim ❖ This explanation is a bit complex, so bear with me!

Some rose varieties have different numbers of chromosomes than others. Roses with the regular complement of chromosomes are called diploids. Those with double the usual number of chromosomes are called tetraploids. When a diploid species crosses with a tetraploid, the resultant seeds are triploid. Triploid seeds are often sterile.

The only way to produce a rose that is identical to the parent plant is to take cuttings from the parent (unless it is a species rose). Because the cutting is simply a piece of the parent, the two are genetically identical. Seeds, on the other hand, often contain genetic material from two distinct parents, and produce variable results.

What does "true to type" mean?

Jim ❖ This simply means that the offspring will be identical to the parent. If a species rose self-pollinates, or cross-pollinates with another rose from the same species, the resulting seed is "true to type"—it produces plants nearly identical to the parents.

Because nearly all cultivars have mixed backgrounds, however, the only way to produce true-to-type offspring is to take cuttings.

Will roses reseed themselves?

Jim ❖ Wild species roses can reseed themselves, but it's unlikely to happen with the roses in your garden, for all the reasons listed in the last several questions.

Cuttings

If I can't grow roses from seed, how do I propagate them?

Jim ❖ If you're adventurous and patient, you can take cuttings from your plants and root them, or you can graft one rose onto another. Almost all commercially available roses are propagated this way.

How do I take root cuttings from my roses?

Jim ❖ Here are the basic steps to follow to grow your own roses from cuttings.

- When the blooms begin to fade, take pencil-thick cuttings using half-hardened wood (newer growth, but not the newest).
- At this point, if you took the cuttings in the fall, store them in a cooler until the following spring.
- Dip each cutting in a rooting compound and shake off any excess.
- Insert the cut end into sterile potting mix and place the entire cutting in a plastic bag.
- Leave the bag in a bright spot (but not in direct sun).
- Check often for moisture and add water as needed.
- Once the roots are several centimetres long, transplant the cuttings into pots and begin fertilizing them weekly with 10-52-10.
- It will take at least 4 weeks for your cuttings to root well.

Cabbage Rose—double flower, old garden rose

When is the best time to propagate my roses?

Lois ❖ You can take cuttings in the fall, but you'll have more success if you take your cuttings as early in the growing season as possible. This gives your new plants more time to establish themselves before winter.

Jim ❖ Although you can take cuttings in the fall and store them over the winter, I recommend that home gardeners do it in the spring. Take cuttings from half-hardened wood, but don't leave it too late in the season. If the cuttings don't have time to root well, they won't survive the winter.

Be sure to take cuttings only from roses grown on their own roots (the Explorer roses are all good choices). Keep in mind, though, that the large potted roses you see in the stores have been grown for a full year or two, so be patient. Propagating roses is slow, but many rosarians find it both enjoyable and rewarding.

Can I divide roses?

Lois ❖ No. If you try to divide roses, you'll severely injure them.

Jim ❖ Instead, try air layering your roses. This works well for hardy roses with flexible stems.

Bring a branch down to the ground and cover part of it—including at least one node (bud)—with good, fertile soil. Use bricks to hold the branch in place while it roots. The tip of the stem sticking out of the soil will eventually grow into a new plant. Once the new plant has rooted, you can cut the stem connecting it to the mother plant and move your new rose to a new location.

This process can be very slow, and doesn't work for all varieties, but give it a try!

Grower's edge

Another Air Layering Method

This method stimulates root formation in plants that are difficult to grow from cuttings.

1. After scoring out two rings half an inch apart on the stem, peel off the bark between them.

2. Brush the stripped area of the stem with a thin dusting of #1 rooting powder.

3. Wrap the bottom of an oblong sheet of plastic tightly around the stem, tying it with thread.

4. Fill the cup-like piece of plastic with moistened sphagnum moss. Close the cup and secure it.

5. When roots appear through the moss, remove the plastic and cut the stem below the roots.

6. Place the new root ball in a pot, and work in potting mixture all around the root.

Grafting

What is grafting?

Lois ❖ Simply put, grafting connects two pieces of living plant in such a way that they "knit" together and grow as one plant. In roses, this usually involves grafting the stem or bud of one variety onto the root of another.

Jim ❖ Grafting has gradually fallen out of favour, particularly in the north. For decades, northern rosarians have grafted stems from tender roses onto roots from hardy ones, in order to help the tender roses survive the winter. Now, however, most no longer believe that grafting confers hardiness. More often, the tender portion of the plant dies back in winter and is replaced by shoots from the rootstock the following spring. As a result, most northern gardeners now steer away from grafted roses.

Miss All-American Beauty—double flower, hybrid tea, good long-stemmed cutflower

grafted rose

What is a rootstock?

Jim ❖ Rootstock is any rose root grown specifically to have other roses
grafted onto it. There are different rootstocks for different purposes.
North American cutflower greenhouse producers use *Rosa manetti* and
Rosa odorata, because those roots provide high shoot numbers plus the
right stem length for cutflowers. For garden roses, the rootstock most
often used in North America is *Rosa multiflora,* because of its hardiness,
while in Europe *Rosa canina* is preferred.

Why are roses grafted?

Jim ❖ The rose industry still uses grafting to propagate roses because it is
an efficient and inexpensive method—especially for new cultivars—and
to take advantage of pest-resistant rootstock. Most rosarians, however,
prefer "own root" roses—roses grown on their own roots—particularly
for northern gardens where winter-hardiness is of greater importance.

How is the bud joined to the rootstock?

Jim ❖ This is a process known as "T-budding." First, the grower cuts the
main stem of the rootstock 5–25 cm above soil level, where the bark is
smooth. He or she then makes a vertical cut through the top of the stem,
about 3 cm deep, and a small horizontal cut—forming an inverted "T."
The grower then inserts the new bud into the cut, and binds the stem
with wrapping material. This area is called the "bud union."

Can I graft my own roses?

Lois ❖ There's really no reason for most gardeners to bother grafting their
own roses. However, if you're interested in experimenting, be sure to do
your research and go right ahead!

Carrot Top—double flower, miniature

Containers

Can I grow a hybrid tea rose in a pot on my deck or balcony during the summer?

Lois ❖ Yes, you can grow any rose in a container, provided the container is large enough. I prefer hybrid tea roses because they produce so many large fragrant flowers. Just make sure to use good potting soil, and to give your rose plenty of sun, warmth, water, and fertilizer.

Jim ❖ Miniature roses do particularly well in containers. Consider trailing varieties like the Flowercarpet Series, or other heavy bloomers such as Gourmet Popcorn and Weeping China Doll.

How big should my container be?

Lois ❖ For young rosebushes, a minimum 21-cm pot works best—any less than this and your rose will quickly overgrow its container. Later in the summer, you'll have to transplant your rose into a 27-cm pot, unless it's a miniature variety.

Jim ❖ Roses consume a large amount of moisture and fertilizer so it's particularly important to grow them in large containers. If you put a mature rosebush into anything smaller than a 27-cm pot, you won't be able to keep up with the watering. Your rose will be less vigourous and produce fewer blooms.

Graham Thomas—double flower, English rose

What type of pot should I choose for my rose?

Lois ❖ By and large, any pot is suitable as long as it's big enough. Remember, though, that soil dries out more quickly in clay pots, because they're porous. You'll have to water more often than you would with plastic or sealed clay pots.

Jim ❖ Consider spending a few extra dollars for an attractive container, particularly if your plant will be located in a focal point in your yard. A nice pot really adds to the display and can be reused for years to come.

If you need to leave your roses on their own for several days at a time, you might be best off with a self-watering pot. A self-watering pot includes a reservoir for extra water, which it then wicks up gradually into the soil. If you fill the reservoir before a weekend getaway, you can enjoy your trip without worrying about your roses. Don't use a saucer outside; if the excess water can't drain away, your roses may end up with root rot.

Can I grow roses in a four-season sunroom?

Lois ❖ You can, provided that the sunroom mimics a rose's preferred natural environment: plenty of sun, not too much heat.

Jim ❖ Even in a sunroom, your roses may not get adequate light during the winter, because the days are shorter and the light is less intense. Roses only bloom when they get plenty of light. In fact, commercial producers often use HID lamps 24 hours a day to keep their hybrid teas blooming profusely. At the same time, though, roses don't like hot weather—they prefer temperatures around 16–24°C.

If you can find this combination of bright, plentiful light and cool temperatures in your home, you can try growing your roses indoors.

The challenge doesn't end there, unfortunately. At some point in the winter, your roses need a two-month period of dormancy. You'll have to find a cold, dark space to store them in—ideally, just a degree or two above freezing.

Little Artist—semi-double flower, miniature

Flower Girl   semi-double flower, floribunda

Can I overwinter my rose in its container?

Jim ❖ In areas with harsh winters like here in Alberta, your container rose
will only survive the winter outdoors if you bury it. Water your rose
thoroughly, wrap it in cloth or burlap to keep it clean, and lay the pot
and plant sideways in a trench. Bury it completely and add a layer of
compost or peat moss for extra protection. Finally, mark the spot so
you can find your rose next spring!

Soil is a great insulator. Even during a prairie cold snap, the chill doesn't
penetrate deep into the soil. By burying your rose on its side, you protect
the entire plant, canes and all.

To overwinter a container rose indoors, move it in the late fall to a cool,
dark place (-5–0°C). Check it periodically throughout the winter, and add
just enough water to keep it from drying out completely. In late January
or early February, move it to a warm, bright location and begin watering
and fertilizing.

Transplanting

When can I transplant my roses?

Lois ❖ You can transplant container-grown roses (leafed out and well rooted) any time from spring (after the danger of severe cold) until late fall—three to four weeks before the first heavy frosts.

Jim ❖ Make sure to allow each rose enough space to accommodate it when it matures. During warm spells, it's best to plant in the early morning or evening. Your plants can dry out quickly on hot, windy afternoons.

Bare-root, boxed, and bagged roses require a little bit more care. You must plant them in the spring, to allow them a full growing season to get established.

To relocate a rose, dig it up in the early spring, just as the new shoots begin to swell. By moving it before it begins to grow actively, you give it the entire growing season to re-establish itself in its new location.

Grower's edge

1. Dig a planting hole that is wider and deeper than the container in which the rose is growing. Mix lots of organic matter—peat moss, compost or well-rotted manure— with the soil. Stir in a handful or two of bone meal (see p. 66), to aid root development.

2. Remove the rosebush from its pot. Gently untangle the rootball to enable the roots to spread into the soil as the rosebush grows.

3. Set the rose into the planting hole.

4. Refill the planting hole with your mix of soil and organic matter, and firmly pack the soil around the stem, leaving a small depression around the base of the rosebush.

5. Water until soil is completely soaked. Newly planted rosebushes should be watered regularly and thoroughly once a week during first growing season. Fertilize once a month with 20-20-20 until the first of August.

Lynn Anderson—double flower, hybrid tea

Do roses suffer from transplant shock? How do you prevent it?

Lois ❖ Well-rooted, conditioned potted roses suffer essentially no transplant shock. Just remember to water and fertilize them properly. This is particularly important with new transplants, because the roots haven't penetrated into the soil.

Jim ❖ Small packaged roses or bare-root roses suffer the most transplant shock. Water each bush well after planting, then hill it up with soil, leaving only the last $\frac{1}{4}$–$\frac{1}{2}$ of the branches showing. Keep the soil moist, and remove the hill two weeks later.

What is hardening off?

Lois ❖ When you harden off a plant, you allow it to gradually adjust to outdoor conditions. If you take a rose directly from a cosy greenhouse in the spring and plant it in your garden, it suffers from the shock of the transition. Most nurseries harden off their roses in the spring before selling them.

Jim ❖ Roses also undergo a hardening off process in the fall. The soft tissues gradually harden in preparation for the coming winter. To aid this process, stop adding nitrogen fertilizers 10–12 weeks before the ground freezes, and water less frequently. As well, stop deadheading finished blooms and allow the plant to set rose hips. This triggers the plant to harden off for winter.

How do you harden off roses in the spring?

Jim ❖ Once temperatures rise above freezing, put your roses outside in a sheltered spot during the day. Bring them in at night if there's a threat of frost. Outdoors, your roses receive far more light than they would indoors, and the cool temperatures and wind harden them off.

How long can I keep roses in my garage before planting?

Lois ❖ Unless it's bitterly cold, you're better off planting your roses in the ground as soon as possible. If you must keep your roses in the garage temporarily, be sure to put them outdoors during the day. They won't receive nearly enough light in the garage. Remember to check every day to see if they need to be watered.

Jim ❖ If you keep your roses in the garage, they'll send out weak, spindly shoots. At the greenhouse, we call this condition "Garage Plant Syndrome."

Outdoors, even on a cloudy day, your roses get at least twice as much sunlight as they do indoors, even next to a sunny window. At the same time, the outside conditions help harden them off for transplanting.

Intensity (fc) of different light sources

Light Source	Location	fc (foot candle*)
Sunlight	outdoors–full sun	10,000
	greenhouse– winter overcast	1,000
	home indoors:	
	1 ft from north window	200–500
	3 ft from north window	100–180
	1 ft from south window–shade	500–900
	1 ft from east window	250–400
	2 ft from east or west window	150–250

* Foot candles is a unit of measurement that is rapidly becoming obsolete in the greenhouse industry. The new term is micromoles per square metre per second and is abbreviated $\mu mol/m^{-2}/s^{-1}$. The approximate conversion to fc is to divide foot candles by 5 to get micromoles.

How deep should I plant my rose?

Lois ❖ Assuming your rose isn't grafted, simply plant it at the same level as the soil in the pot.

Jim ❖ If your rose is grafted, plant the graft 10 cm below soil level (in climates warmer than zone 3, you don't need to plant it quite as deeply). During the summer, leave a basin in the soil, with the graft barely covered. In the fall, fill the basin in.

Should I soak my roses before transplanting them?

Jim ❖ Treat your roses just like any other potted shrubs and water them thoroughly both before and after transplanting. If you buy bare-root or packaged roses, be careful to keep the roots moist, and plant them as soon as possible.

How far apart should I plant my rose bushes?

Lois ❖ If you want a nice, full look to your flower bed, check the tags to find out how wide the bushes are expected to grow, and leave that amount of space between plants. In other words, if you plant a variety that grows to 1 m in width, plant the bushes at least 1 m apart. To me, roses are always more attractive when they are properly spaced.

Jim ❖ You can space tender roses more closely, because they have an upright growth habit. Tender roses can look a little bare at the bottom if you space them too widely. Leave 75 cm between plants.

Also, if you're planting a hardy rose hedge, take Mom's formula and divide it in half. In other words, if you expect your plants to grow 1 m wide, plant the main stems 50 cm apart so the roots will have enough room to grow, but bushes will eventually grow together to form a hedge. Remember that proper spacing allows sunlight to reach all around the plant and aids in air circulation. If roses are spaced too closely, they will also compete for nutrients and moisture.

Should I grow my roses in a separate bed the way I see them in botanical gardens and parks or can I mix them with other plants?

Lois ❖ With hardy roses, it's purely a matter of taste. Grow them separately or mix them into your beds like any other shrub. In Canada, most people grow tender roses in separate beds. This makes them easier to care for during the growing season and easier to mulch in the fall. If you prefer to mix them in with other plants, go right ahead—it just means you'll have to do a bit of extra work tending individual rosebushes.

Should I cut the blooms on my roses when I transplant them?

Lois ❖ As long as the rose was grown in a pot and has vigourous roots, you don't need to remove any flowers.

Jim ❖ Don't prune branches or roots—the plant should already have been cut back when you bought it. Simply prune off any dead or broken branches.

On packaged roses, however, remove any blooms to allow the plant to devote its energy to establishing leaves and roots, rather than hips.

I've often read about pruning roots and canes prior to planting to "balance" roses. I have yet to see any benefit from this practice. I don't recommend removing any healthy growth from your roses, either roots or canes.

Should I fertilize my roses after transplanting?

Lois ❖ Yes, but don't fertilize container-grown roses excessively. Add more fertilizer as the plant begins to produce lots of new growth.

Jim ❖ Bare-root and boxed roses in particular do need an extra boost when you transplant them. Fertilize them with 10-52-10, once a week for three weeks, to help the roots becomes established. Then, during the main growing season, switch to general purpose 20-20-20 or a good rose fertilizer.

When is the latest I can plant hardy roses in the fall?

Lois ❖ Plant bare root or packaged hardy roses no later than the early summer to allow the roots to fully develop and establish before winter. Potted hardy roses can be planted 3–4 weeks prior to fall freeze-up because they already have large, well-developed root systems.

CHAPTER 4 🌾
THE GROWING SEASON

Some roses are so tough that they need little care to thrive. We had a cluster of Hansa roses in our yard that used to take all kinds of abuse. Bill and Jim and their friends used to play football in that yard, and often used the rosebushes as goalposts or even silent, immobile linesmen. Whenever there was a collision, the Hansas usually emerged with fewer bruises than the players!

Of course, most rose varieties demand more consideration than that. Roses are heavy feeders, requiring extra water and fertilizer to really do their best. And very few of them tolerate contact sports.

The relationship between you and your roses is like any other relationship: what you get out of it largely depends on what you're willing to put into it. If you spend enough time with your roses, and look after their needs, you'll all live happily ever after!

Water

How often should I water my roses?

Lois ❖ Check your roses regularly (every day if you can), and water thoroughly if the surface of the soil is dry. Provided your soil drains well, it's not easy to over-water your roses.

Be sure to give your roses at least one heavy soaking every four or five days. I like to use a flood nozzle which provides a soft, heavy flow of water.

Jim ❖ Ideally, roses should get 3 cm of rainfall per week. In practice, apply about 20 L per bush every week; the moisture should penetrate 30 to 45 cm down into the soil.

Can I use my sprinkler system on my roses?

Lois ❖ Technically yes, but I wouldn't recommend it. You should avoid getting water on the leaves of your roses. I always recommend a water wand with a good flood nozzle for all your plants. A water wand allows you to water your roses just where they need it, at the soil level. Also, it gives you more control over the amount of water you give your plants.

Jim ❖ Sprinklers help prevent infestations of spider mites, but increase the threat of blackspot and grey mould. Also, when you use a sprinkler, much of the water stays on the foliage and evaporates before it can get to the roots.

To get water right to the roots, use a flood nozzle like Mom says. Water in the morning, to allow the foliage to dry quickly. If you don't have time for the hands-on approach, consider investing in soaker hoses or a drip-irrigation system to avoid getting water on the leaves.

Do you recommend watering at any particular time of day?

Lois ❖ I prefer to water my plants first thing in the morning. That way, the water soaks into the soil, instead of evaporating in the hot sun. It also means that if I inadvertently spray the foliage, it will dry before evening. Best of all, watering in the morning means that you start your day with a visit to the rose garden when the fragrance is strongest!

Wild roses grow in hot and dry areas and nobody ever waters them. Why should I bother watering mine?

Lois ❖ If you've spent any time around wild roses, you know that some years they bloom like crazy, and other years hardly at all. The difference lies in the amount of rainfall. If we've had a nice, moist season, you can expect to see thousands of blossoms.

Wild roses depend on nature to provide them with water. Some years, nature lets them down. Garden roses, on the other hand, depend on you for the extra water they need. Get out there with your water wand, and they'll repay you for your kindness!

Jim ❖ Some roses can survive without any irrigation, but they won't be lush and vigorous, or produce many flowers.

Many garden roses are hybrids derived from species that originated in moist environments, while native roses evolved in a somewhat drier environment.

Even wild roses prefer moist soil. That's why you see so many of them in ditches, where the moisture collects. It's also why they tend to flower only in the spring, when they have moist soil and cool temperatures. Once the weather heats up and the soil dries out, they stop flowering.

How often should I water a rose in a container?

Lois ❖ Water your potted rose daily—you'll be surprised at how quickly it dries out, especially as the plant becomes larger and the temperatures rise. Always water until the soil is thoroughly soaked. Don't stop until water begins running out the bottom of the pot. If you use a large pot, you won't have to water as often.

Jim ❖ Remember not to use saucers for patio rose pots. Excess water will collect during rainfalls and rot the roots. Some containers and pots have reservoirs that will store water away from the roots.

Are there any drought-tolerant roses?

Lois ❖ The Alberta wild rose and the hardy Rugosa roses grow well in drier locations, though they don't bloom as much. Spinosas are another good choice.

Fertilizer

How often should I fertilize my roses?
What kind of fertilizer should I use?

Lois ❖ I always say that nothing beats a pinch of good, all-purpose (20-20-20) fertilizer every time you water.

Jim ❖ You can use granular or liquid fertilizer, whichever you prefer. If you choose granular, apply it three times during the growing season: in the spring, late June, and late July. If you prefer a liquid fertilizer, apply it once a week—or every time you water, if you use Mom's "a pinch per watering can" formula.

I prefer to combine the two methods. I give my roses a light dose of granular fertilizer three times during the growing season, and add a bit of liquid fertilizer every time I water.

Either way, stop fertilizing in early August (or slightly later in warmer climates). This prevents the development of soft new growth late in the growing season and signals your plants to begin preparing for winter.

Grower's edge

Symptoms of Nutrient Deficiency

Nitrogen deficiency
• The foliage is yellow-green, particularly the older leaves; this is most noticeable on varieties that normally have dark-green foliage
• The new leaves appear to be stunted

Phosphorus deficiency
• Overall stunting of the plant
• Loss of luster in the old leaves, which become grey-green
• Reduced root development
• Poor flowers

Potassium deficiency
• Marginal browning of leaves
• Deformed flower buds
• Stunted growth

Iron deficiency
• New growth is veiny

Magnesium deficiency
• Older growth is veiny

Sulphur deficiency
• Similar to a nitrogen deficiency—overall growth is pale

What do the three numbers on the fertilizer label mean?

Lois ❖ Nitrogen, phosphorus, and potassium (or N-P-K). The three numbers on a fertilizer package (e.g., 20-20-20) tell you how much of each of these components it contains.

Jim ❖ Fertilizer often contains micronutrients, and other compounds, but the three main elements are nitrogen, phosphorus, and potassium. The numbers translate into percentages. In other words, 20-20-20 fertilizer contains at least 20% nitrogen, 20% phosphate, and 20% potash by weight.

Fertilizers deliver those elements in chemical compounds, rather than in their pure form. You'd have a hard time incorporating pure nitrogen into your fertilizer, for instance, since it's a gas! In a compound like nitrate (NO_3), the nitrogen only makes up about 30% of the molecular weight (the rest is oxygen). That's one of the reasons why, when you add up the 20%+20%+20%, you don't get 100%.

Are roses heavy feeders—do they require a lot of fertilizer to grow well?

Lois ❖ Yes, especially tender roses, if you want plenty of flowers.

Jim ❖ Because roses are such heavy feeders, you want to make sure that they don't have to compete for nutrients. When planting, be sure to leave adequate space around each plant. Also, don't forget to weed!

What are the best fertilizers for my roses?

Lois ❖ I simply use All–Purpose 20-20-20. I also add compost and manure to condition the soil (supply long-term nutrients) and to help my soil retain moisture.

Jim ❖ You can also buy fertilizer specially formulated for roses (I use 28-14-14). There are many good rose fertilizers which usually include chelated iron. This prevents iron deficiency, a common problem for roses.

Can I use lawn fertilizer on my roses?

Lois ❖ It's not a good idea—some lawn fertilizer contains herbicide! Your roses would be much better off with a more balanced fertilizer.

Jim ❖ I don't recommend it. Lawn fertilizers contain a large amount of nitrogen relative to phosphorus and potassium, so it tends to trigger excessively lush foliage at the expense of flower and root development. High nitrogen can also make roses more vulnerable to aphid and mite damage, as well as winterkill.

Can I grow roses organically?

Lois ❖ It is possible, but like any organic gardening, it requires extra work and vigilance.

Jim ❖ The two biggest hurdles in organic gardening are supplying your plants with adequate nutrients and fending off pests and disease.

Because you're not adding chemical fertilizers, it's particularly important that you start off with good soil, rich in organic matter. Work plenty of compost and well-rotted manure into your bed before planting, and add extra from time to time around the base of your plants.

Make sure your roses get plenty of sunlight, water, and air circulation, and you'll go a long way in preventing disease and pest problems. If you do encounter some pests, such as aphids or spider mites, you can often kill them with natural insecticidal soaps, or knock them off of your plants with a blast of water.

Jean Giono—double flower, hybrid tea

Snow Bride—semi-double flower, miniature

What's the difference between organic and chemical fertilizer?

Jim ❖ All fertilizers are actually "chemical" fertilizers, in that they deliver the same elements and compounds to your plants. However, organic and non-organic fertilizers differ in the way they deliver these nutrients.

When you add manure to your soil, for example, microorganisms in the soil digest it. When those organisms die, they release the separate compounds such as ammonium, nitrates, phosphates, and iron oxides. Chemical fertilizers, such as 20-20-20, also contain ammonium, iron, phosphates, and so on. Unlike organic fertilizers, however, they don't have to be broken down before releasing nutrients to the plant. They also contain a much higher concentration of nutrients than organic fertilizers.

In either case, the plant eventually absorbs the same compounds in the same form, whether from an organic or inorganic source.

Keep in mind, however, that organic fertilizers provide more than short-term benefit to your plants. Because they take time to break down, they provide a long-term reservoir of nutrients in your soil. Compost and manure also improve your soil's texture and moisture retention.

My friend doesn't use bone meal on her roses anymore because she's worried about mad-cow disease. Should I be worried too?

Jim ❖ I wouldn't worry. There's no compelling reason to consider bone meal unsafe, particularly in North America. We sell it at our greenhouse, and I don't hesitate to handle it myself. When mixed into the soil around roses, bone meal provides an excellent but very slow-release source of phosphorus.

In 1996, England suffered a higher than usual incidence of Creutzfeldt-Jakob disease (CJD), a fatal brain disorder that normally strikes one person per million each year. Scientists believe the problem was linked to an epidemic of bovine spongiform encephalopathy (mad-cow disease) in English cattle.

Some people fear that they risk exposure to mad-cow disease when they handle bone meal. However, to date no North American study has found any connection between CJD and bone meal.

I heard that if I cut up banana peels and put them into my soil, my roses will be more vibrantly coloured. Is this true?

Lois ❖ Not really, but it doesn't hurt. Banana peels contain lots of potassium. They're a great addition to your compost pile. Roses require a lot of potassium, so I don't hesitate to dig a few banana peels in around my rosebushes.

Jim ❖ In garden soil, the addition of a few banana peels won't have a large impact. You're better off tossing them in the compost pile. If your soil is deficient in potassium, however, banana peels will help a bit—but they won't completely solve the problem.

Roses deficient in potassium typically have stunted growth, shorter flower stems, deformed flower buds, and yellowing or browning of older leaf levels. Potassium deficiency has also been suspected of causing "blind" shoots—shoots that fail to produce flowerbuds, and flowerbuds that fail to open. If you've noticed any of these symptoms in your own roses, you might try digging some banana peels into your soil, but you are better off to add the needed potassium in the form of a fertilizer. Just put those peels in the compost. 15-15-30 fertilizer has 30% potash, which is excellent for potassium-deficient soil.

Can I use eggshells in my rose bed?

Lois ❖ Eggshells add a bit of extra calcium to your soil, but they are not a replacement for regular fertilizer. Eggshells will likely have little effect on your roses—but on the other hand, they won't hurt!

Jim ❖ Most soil already contains enough calcium. If you do add eggshells to your soil or to your compost, be sure they're dry. Otherwise, they may attract animals.

Elina—double flower, hybrid tea

Growing Indoors

Can I grow roses under lights indoors?

Lois ❖ Yes, but roses require lots of light. I tell most people to grow their roses outdoors, either in containers or in the garden. If you really want to try growing roses indoors under lights, stick with the miniature varieties and use special grow lights.

Jim ❖ Roses are usually only grown indoors in commercial greenhouses. Even there, the grow lights only supplement the natural light—they don't provide all of it.

The standard grow lights you can purchase at a garden centre won't provide sufficient light for vigourous, healthy plants. You need lights specifically designed for growing roses and other similar plants. High-intensity discharge lights (HID) provide lots of light; however, they're much too bulky and expensive for a home environment.

Can I grow miniature roses indoors?

Lois ❖ Indoors, your miniature roses won't receive enough light to grow well, particularly in the winter. They also prefer cooler temperatures than we do—16-18°C. In short, if I were looking for a flowering houseplant, I'd choose something else!

Maintenance

Do I need to clean up the petals and leaves as they fall off my rose bush?

Lois ❖ It's a good idea. The cleaner the area, the better it looks. Also, a clean area helps protect your plant's health.

Jim ❖ Cleaning up reduces the chance that pests and diseases will spread; for example, the larvae of the rose weevil grow inside rose buds. Roses also produce more blooms if you remove the faded or finished flowers.

Fungal spores and harmful insects just love hanging around in dead plant material. When you clean up the area, they have fewer places to hide.

If your plants have any blackspot or mildew, place the infected leaves in your garbage—not in your compost pile! Otherwise, you risk spreading the disease.

Should I cultivate around my roses?

Lois ❖ Yes, but be careful. Roses have shallow root systems and can be easily damaged by deep tillage.

Jim ❖ You must cultivate around your roses in order to control weeds. As long as you don't penetrate more than a few centimetres beneath the surface, you won't damage the roots.

Should I use weed barrier on my roses?

Lois ❖ It's not necessary, but some people like to use it to minimize their weed problems. Weed barriers are woven fabrics that allow moisture through yet keep weeds from penetrating the surface.

Jim ❖ Be sure to clean off any organic material that accumulates on the fabric surface. Otherwise, weeds will eventually sprout on it and send roots down through the fabric.

Deadheading

What is deadheading?

Lois ❖ Deadheading is the removal of dead flowers. It encourages your roses to keep blooming, and also makes them look tidier.

Jim ❖ By removing the dead flowers from your rosebush, you prevent your plant from producing seed (contained in the rosehips). Seed production signals your plant to reduce bloom production. As well, the seed also draws away a lot of energy that would otherwise go into new growth and new flowers.

How do I deadhead roses without damaging them?

Lois ❖ Simply clip off the flowers as soon as they begin to droop. Use sharp pruners—a clean cut leaves your plant less vulnerable to disease. I don't recommend regular scissors because they are difficult to use and don't cut as cleanly as pruners.

Do I have to deadhead my roses?

Lois ❖ Roses don't require deadheading—in fact, if you're growing roses for the hips, it's the last thing you want to do. You also don't need to deadhead varieties that bloom only once per season, although I prefer to remove the faded blooms because it's easier than cleaning up fallen petals. For repeat-blooming varieties, though, I recommend regular deadheading.

When should I stop deadheading my roses?

Lois ❖ Stop deadheading about six weeks before the first killing frost in your area. For me, that usually means stopping near the end of August. This gives your rose plenty of time to form hips and harden off.

Jim ❖ It's important to eventually allow the hips to form, because this signals your rose to acclimatize prior to the onset of winter. If you don't allow your roses to gradually harden off, you lower their chances of surviving through the long, cold months ahead.

Pruning

What can I do to keep my hardy rose bushes tidy?

Lois ❖ First, thin out the rose bushes by removing the weaker growth. To grow the best roses possible, you're much better off with fewer strong canes than many smaller ones. Next, remove any diseased or dying canes. Not only will your rosebush be healthier, it will also look more attractive.

I've always heard that you should prune to an outward-facing bud, but I'm not sure exactly what that means.

Lois ❖ To encourage your bush to spread nicely, you want to choose buds that face out from the plant. Otherwise, the new branches will grow in upon one another. This makes the bush look untidy, and prevents sunlight from reaching many of the leaves.

Jim: ❖ Remember to always cut just above a bud. Before you remove a cane, find a 5-leaflet leaf near where you want to cut (see drawing). Immediately above the spot where the leaf joins the branch (the axil), you'll find a tiny bud. After you prune, that's where your cane will send out a new shoot.

Make your cut ½ cm above the bud; otherwise you may injure or dehydrate it. Many people believe that you should prune rose canes at a 45° angle to shed water, but I always cut mine straight across and they grow just fine.

I don't know which branches to prune!

Lois ❖ If you're growing tender roses in a cold climate, you often need to remove only damaged or diseased branches.

Jim ❖ Inspect and prune your hardy rosebushes in the spring. First, remove any dead canes, plus any broken or diseased canes. Then, if your bush is at least three years old, remove one quarter to one third of your canes. Look for the oldest, thickest canes, and snip them off right at ground level.

If you've got a lot of inward-growing or crossed branches, remove them. Not only do they look bad, they provide a sheltered environment for growth of disease. Remember to prune to outward-facing buds.

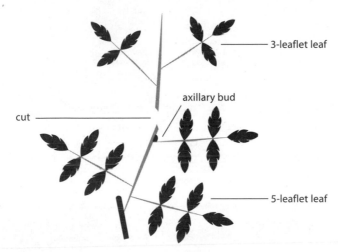

How should I prune my climbing rose?

Lois ❖ For the first two or three years, don't prune it at all! Just remove dead branches in the spring. After that, use your pruning to shape the bush, encouraging it to spread outwards and upwards on the support.

Should I prune my miniature rose?

Lois ❖ Miniature roses are so easy to grow! They require very little maintenance, including pruning. Deadhead them and remove any dead branches, but apart from that they don't require any pruning. Some growers like to gently shear their miniature roses to maintain their shape, but it's a matter of taste.

Jim ❖ Miniature roses don't need much pruning because they were specifically bred to remain small and compact. Just cut off the faded blooms, and keep an eye open for any dead or diseased wood to remove.

When I prune my tree rose, should I do anything differently?

Lois ❖ You want to ensure that all the new branches are formed in the top portion of the bush. Remove any new growth from the base or main stem as soon as it appears. As with miniature roses, some people like to prune their tree roses to maintain a "ball" shape. Don't allow the ball to get too large unless you stake the cane.

Is it better to prune my roses in the fall or in the spring?

Lois ❖ It depends whether they are tender or hardy. Prune your hardy roses in the early spring, as soon as the new leaves begin to unfurl. That way, your plant has a full season to grow.

Jim ❖ There's an added benefit to spring-pruning your hardy roses. Although they do experience some die-back or tip kill during harsh winters, after a mild winter you will see new growth right to the tips. By keeping this growth intact, you end up with a bigger bush.

With tender roses, cut them back to 30 cm each fall after they become dormant. This makes them easier to mulch and reduces overwintering diseases. When you uncover them in the spring, bring along your shears and snip off any dead canes.

Happy Child—double flower, English rose

What kind of pruners should I use on my roses?

Lois ❖ Anvil pruners crush the stems, so use only bypass shears.

Be prepared to invest in good quality. If you've ever been to one of my gardening talks, you've heard me relate my favourite Grandma Hole quote: "Only the rich can afford to buy cheap things."

Top-quality, carbon steel secateurs last far longer than the so-called "bargain brands" and don't need sharpening as often. By spending those few extra dollars, you'll make your life so much easier. You'll notice the difference with every cut you make.

If I prune my hardy rose too severely in the early spring, will it look bad all summer?

Lois ❖ Assuming your bush was well established, it will bounce back in no time. In fact, it may end up looking better than ever.

Jim ❖ You can prune back a rose quite severely, and it will grow back surprisingly quickly. I don't recommend that treatment, however!

If you have neglected your pruning for a few years, don't try to catch up all at once. Make it a two-year project. Do a bit of extra pruning this spring, and some more next spring. That way, you spare your plant the trauma of a single severe pruning session.

Winter Protection

How do I protect tender roses over the winter?

Jim ❖ After the frost has killed off the foliage, cut your rose back to 30 cm from ground level and water it thoroughly. Once the surface of the soil has dried, cover it with at least 30 cm of peat moss (you can also use rose huts, which are essentially oversized styrofoam cups). Cover the peat moss with a bit of soil, to ensure that it doesn't blow away. During the winter, throw a few shovels full of extra snow on top of your mulch, to add an extra layer of insulation.

One 3.8 cubic foot bale of peat moss covers about eight to ten bushes. You can also use fiberglass, anchored with wire or burlap, or a thick layer of straw. Some people even use old carpets! Powder the plant with sulphur before mulching, to prevent disease and discourage rodents.

Painted Moon—double flower, hybrid tea, good cutflower

Can I bring my tender roses inside during the winter?

Lois ❖ You can, provided you've got the right place to store them. If you have a cold room or garage where the temperature stays within a few degrees of freezing, it's well worth a try. Check them from time to time throughout the winter, and water them just enough to keep them from drying out completely.

Jim ❖ You can bring them inside, as long as the temperatures are cool enough but not too cold. You want to keep your roses in a dormant state without freezing them. If roses get too warm (greater than 5°C) they begin to grow and "burn out," because they use up energy faster than they can obtain it from the limited light indoors. If they get colder than about -5°C for prolonged periods, they may suffer severe damage.

The roses I overwintered in my garage look bad. Now that it's spring, how can I perk them up?

Lois ❖ Put them out in the sun and keep them well watered. A bright, sheltered corner of your deck would be ideal. If they don't show signs of recovery within a couple of weeks, give up on them. Otherwise, keep them constantly outside except when the temperature drops below freezing.

Jim ❖ If the buds are firm and green, but not growing, the environment was just right. But if the plants have produced lots of soft shoots, the garage was too warm. In this case, do as Mom says—place the roses on a sheltered deck, keep the soil moist, and hope for the best!

Spring

How do I know when to uncover my tender roses in the spring?

Jim ❖ Don't be too hasty—tender roses are more likely to be killed by the freeze/thaw cycles of spring and fall than by the -30°C winters. Once the buds on native trees and shrubs start to swell, it's time to uncover your roses. Well-conditioned roses, even the tender varieties, can withstand several degrees of frost.

Jayne Austin—double flower, English rose

Will plastic clear covers (or cloches) promote early blooms on my roses?

Jim ❖ The length of time before your plant blooms depends on temperature and light levels. As temperature increases, the metabolism of the plant speeds up. Covering your rose bushes with a clear plastic sheet allows the heat to build up, signalling your plants to begin flowering.

Before covering your roses, though, consider these potential problems:

• With the plastic trapping the heat, roses can easily overheat, even on cool days.

• Because the plant tissue hasn't been hardened off by cool temperatures, your plants will be more vulnerable to cold and pests.

• Plastic does not provide frost protection—it will only help trap heat.

If you remove the plastic cover abruptly, you can set your rose back. Gradually toughen up the softer growth by exposing them to a few more hours of air movement and cool temperatures each day.

CHAPTER 5 ✖
ENJOY ROSES

Like many suitors, my husband-to-be,
Ted, used roses to express his
affection back when we were dating.
As one point in the courtship, Ted
sent me a dozen gorgeous red roses,
along with a card that read, "A bushel
and a peck. Ted." At the time—this
was the early '50s—there was
a popular song that went "I love you
a bushel and a peck…" Ted left the
"I love you" part off the card,
but in my mind I filled it in.

Roses are the most romantic
of flowers, but their use isn't
limited to the art of love. In the
hope that you will enjoy roses to
the fullest, here's a bit of insight
into their amazing versatility.

Cutting Roses

Can I cut roses from my bushes to use for cutflowers?

Lois ❖ Definitely! Nothing beats fresh roses cut from your very own garden. Cut as many as you wish, but stop in the early fall to allow the bushes to begin to harden off for winter.

Jim ❖ If this is the first year your rosebush has been planted, avoid cutting long stems. Remove as few leaves as possible, in order to give your plant a better chance to become well established.

When is the best time of day to cut roses?

Lois ❖ Cut them in the cool of the early morning, when the flowers are fresh and fragrant. I like to keep a few roses in my kitchen—they fill the whole room with fragrance.

Jim ❖ Rose blossoms lose moisture rapidly during the heat of the afternoon. If you cut them in the morning or evening, they're under much less heat stress. Thoroughly water your rosebushes at least a few hours before cutting flowers, to ensure that the blooms contain as much moisture as possible.

Martin Frobisher—double flower, hardy shrub

How can I make my cut roses last longer?

Jim ❖ This is the number-one question in our floral department. In addition to cutting your blooms in the morning, here are a few other tips.

- Bacterial infection can cause your roses to wilt. To prevent infection, rinse your vase thoroughly with a bleach solution to sterilize it, then rinse it again with plain water to remove the bleach residue.

- Before putting the flowers in your vase, re-cut the stems. Always cut the stems underwater to avoid embolisms (trapped air bubbles that prevent water flow within the stems).

- Cut the stems at a 45° angle. This exposes a greater surface area to the water and keeps the ends off the bottom of the vase, allowing the stems to draw water more easily.

- Cut off any foliage that will be below the waterline to prevent rotting.

- Add floral preservative, to supply sugar and prevent bacterial growth.

- Keep your roses in a cool location, away from direct sunlight.

Say it with roses...

In Victorian times, suitors often used the colours of their roses to send subtle, coded messages to the object of their affections. The custom has faded, but hasn't died out completely. We still get a lot of calls from people wanting to know the meanings attached to different colours of roses. Unfortunately, there's no single, universally accepted guide. We can, however, pass along a few of the more popular definitions:

- Red—True love (no surprise there!)
- White—Innocence, purity, and charm
- Yellow—Joy
- Deep pink—Gratitude
- Pale pink—Sympathy and admiration
- Coral/Orange— Enthusiasm and desire

Of course, speaking the "language of roses" only works if the recipient understands what you're trying to say. Most people today judge their colours according to personal preference, rather than hidden meaning. Men traditionally send red roses, yet more women prefer yellow...

If you want to send a clear, easy-to-understand message with your roses, play it safe—write it on a card!

What is the best method to cut roses?

Lois ❖ Cut the stem just above an outward-facing bud. Keep in mind, the longer you cut your stem, the longer it will take for the plant to produce a new stem and flower.

Sometimes, I like to snip off a single flower and float it in a rosebowl. It's a wonderful way to enjoy the flowers from your rose while leaving the foliage on the plant.

Frülingsmorgen—single flower, hardy shrub, can be used as a climber

Drying Roses

How do I air-dry roses?

Lois ❖ Air-drying is the easiest way to dry your roses. Simply hang your roses upside down, either individually or in small bunches. The blooms dry completely in about a week.

Jim ❖ Unfortunately, air-dried roses don't maintain their colours well. Red roses end up looking almost black, while white or soft-coloured roses tend to go slightly brown.

My friend dries roses using silica gel. Where do I get it, and how do I use it?

Lois ❖ A rose dried in silica gel retains its natural shape and colour much better than an air-dried rose. You can purchase silica gel at any good craft store.

Pour a thick bed of gel in the bottom of a box or other container. Lay the individual flowers on the gel, and gently pour more gel around and over them until they're completely buried. Leave them for 5-7 days, then check them carefully to confirm that they have dried completely.

Jim ❖ Dessicants, such as silica gel, attract and hold water molecules. That's why your rose dries out when you bury it in silica, even though there's virtually no air circulation.

Some people achieve almost instant results by combining the silica gel method with drying in a microwave oven. Bury the flower as Mom describes, and then microwave it, box and all, for a minute or so (you'll have to experiment to find the exact times for your particular oven). Take the box out, and leave it undisturbed for half an hour. Carefully check the petals to make sure they're papery-dry.

The great thing about silica gel is that you can reuse it almost indefinitely. If it ever starts to lose its effectiveness, simply place it in a warm oven for an hour or so to evaporate all the moisture.

A few words on behalf of rosehips...

- Roses come from the same plant family as apples, raspberries, and strawberries. Roses are sometimes grown commercially for their fruit—rosehips—rather than their flowers.

- Rosehips contain up to 20 times more vitamin C than oranges. The level goes up the farther north you go from the equator.

- Rugosa roses are often grown for their hips, because they produce lots of edible pulp.

- When citrus fruits became unavailable in England during World War Two, the government ordered the gathering of rosehips to be processed into syrup to prevent scurvy.

Which rose varieties are best for drying?

Lois ❖ You can dry any kind of rose with silica gel. Look for blooms that have opened, but aren't yet "fully blown." Rosebuds also look lovely when dried. Pick the flowers in mid-morning, just after the dew has dried from the petals.

How do I make potpourri?

Lois ❖ Gently pull the petals off your roses, and dry them on wire screens in a well-ventilated room. Dry the petals immediately after cutting the roses—fresh flowers contain more essential oils.

When all of the petals have dried completely, combine them with other fragrant plant material, such as rosemary, lavender, seed pods, dried citrus slices or peel, cloves, and borage flowers. You can also add an extra sprinkling of essential oils.

A bowl of potpourri can add colour and fragrance to a room for months!

Trumpeter—double flower, floribunda

Electron—double flower, hybrid tea

Eating Roses

Are roses edible?

Lois ❖ As you go through life, be sure to take time to stop and eat the roses! All roses and rose hips are edible, provided you haven't treated them with pesticides.

Pick the flowers in the mid-morning, just as you would if you were drying them or putting them in a vase. Choose flowers that have opened fully, but haven't begun to fade.

Jim ❖ People think of edible flowers as a recent craze. In fact, the practice of eating roses was far more widespread in Shakespeare's time than in our own.

Which roses taste best?

Lois ❖ All rose petals are edible, and each variety tastes slightly different. Generally speaking, if a rose smells nice it probably tastes nice. If you're curious, just pluck off a petal and pop it in your mouth! Remember to harvest in the morning.

Rugosa roses are best for jelly, syrup or ice cream, and are also delicious in salads. French rose petals (*Rosa gallica*) make a striking edible garnish. If you are interested in more information, see my book *Herbs & Edible Flowers*.

Can I eat my rose petals after they've been treated with pesticide?

Jim ❖ Since not all of the pesticides used on roses are registered for edible plants, I recommend using **only** untreated rose petals.

What can I do with rosehips? Are they edible?

Some Roses for Showy Rosehips

Adelaide Hoodless
Alba Semi-plena
Celestial
Dart's Dash
Double White Burnet
Frau Dagmar Hartopp
Frühlingsanfang
Frühlingsmorgen
George Vancouver
Hansa
Jens Munk
Kakwa
Louis Jolliet
Morden Centennial
Red Frau Dagmar Hartopp
Red Rugosa
Red-leaf Rose
Scabrosa
Schneezwerg
Sweetbriar Rose
Thérèse Bugnet
White Rugosa

Lois ❖ When I was younger, we ate rosehips during the fall until the frost came. We used to peel the skins off with our teeth and spit out the seeds. Pick them when they're full and red, but before they start to go soft. They're a bit fiddly to prepare. Cut off the stem and blossom ends, and scoop out the fibres and seeds with a spoon.

You can eat prepared rosehips fresh—they taste like very tangy cranberries. You can also use them fresh in recipes, freeze them, or dry them.

Jim ❖ Throughout history, rosehips have often played a crucial role in people's diets, particularly when other vegetables and fruits were in short supply. On a more personal note, I've loved rosehip jam on toast ever since I was a boy.

Adelaide Hoodless—double flower, hardy shrub

CHAPTER 6 ❧
TROUBLESHOOTING

*Mutations, pests, fading blooms, disease,
flowers that refuse to unfurl…each season
seems to bring with it a new difficulty. But
don't let these troubles overwhelm you;
most are easy to rectify, given the right
information. Even that most dreaded nem-
esis, powdery mildew, is fairly easy to fore-
stall if you just keep your roses healthy
with plenty of water and fertilizer.*

Double Delight—double flower, hybrid tea

Roses seem to be especially vulnerable to bugs and disease. Why is that?

Lois ❖ Roses are only slightly more vulnerable than many other plants in your garden. If bugs are damaging your roses, you can control them with insecticides, including insecticidal soap.

Jim ❖ In the case of disease, an ounce of prevention is worth a pound of cure. For instance, certain hybrids are particularly prone to blackspot and powdery mildew. By avoiding those varieties, you can substantially reduce these problems.

What can I do to help my roses resist disease and pest problems?

Lois ❖ No rose is completely immune to problems. However, problems most often strike when plants are in a weakened state. Give your roses adequate water, fertilizer, and sunshine, and you'll keep your disease and pest problems to a minimum.

Jim ❖ Just about any rose can be more resistant to insects and diseases, with a little help. Water, fertilize, and prune your rosebushes. Examine them closely to catch any problem at an early stage. Regularly clear away any fallen leaves or other debris, which can provide a haven for harmful insects and diseases.

Do roses get powdery mildew? How do I prevent it?

Lois ❖ Yes. Powdery mildew is the most troubling disease affecting roses in a northern climate. It often strikes plants that are already stressed for other reasons. Powdery mildew looks like talcum powder sprinkled across the leaves. Treat it right away—it spreads quickly.

Jim ❖ Powdery mildew is a disease that attacks many species of plants. There are many species of powdery mildew as well; however, most species are specific to a certain genus of plants. For example, the mildew that attacks begonias won't attack roses, or vice versa. Powdery mildew spores germinate only on damp leaves. On a cool evening following a hot day, for instance, leaves can become covered by a slight film of dew—providing the ideal environment for mildew spore germination.

Space your bushes, to allow for better air circulation and to help the foliage dry faster.

How does powdery mildew spread?

Jim ❖ The mildew typically begins as tiny spores that land on your leaf—blown there by the wind or splashed from plant to plant by rainfall.

The spores remain dormant until they get the moisture they require to germinate. Once the leaf becomes moist and stays moist for about three hours (say, from overhead sprinkling or condensation on a cool, moist night), the mildew begins to develop. It rapidly spreads in white strands (hyphae) across the face of the leaf, dropping pegs (haustoria) into the leaf to anchor it and allow it to draw nutrients from your plant. After that point, it doesn't need any more leaf-surface moisture to proliferate—it gets all it needs directly from within the leaves.

Powdery mildew tends to attack plants that are already vulnerable for one reason or another. Anything that weakens the plant allows the mildew to penetrate the leaf surface more easily. For instance, plants that don't get enough sunlight tend to have thinner leaves, making them more prone to infection. Plants deficient in nutrients (calcium in particular) have weaker leaf tissue and are also more vulnerable.

Octoberfest—double flower, grandiflora

How do I treat powdery mildew?

Lois ❖ When you spot the first signs, spray your plants with benomyl every seven days, and remove and destroy any affected foliage. Continue giving them enough water and fertilizer.

Jim ❖ Like most diseases, powdery mildew is much easier to treat if you catch it early.

Every day, when you're in your garden, keep an eye open for it. If you spot any infected leaves, remove and destroy them immediately, and begin a program of spraying. Don't delay—once it starts to run rampant, it's nearly impossible to control.

Spray every seven to ten days using benomyl. Some people also like to use baking soda: about 15 mL per 4L of water (1 tablespoon per gallon) combined with a 10% solution of summer plant oil. Always experiment on a few leaves before treating the whole plant to ensure the spray does no damage.

Shady, damp spots in the garden are more prone to mildew—if you have problems, move your rose to a brighter area.

Where should I look for signs of powdery mildew? Which roses are most resistant?

Jim ❖ On any rosebush, the young tissue is most vulnerable; older tissue is less susceptible.

If you've had problems with powdery mildew, try planting Rugosas. In my experience, they're one of the most resistant species.

Which varieties are most resistant to powdery mildew?

Lois ❖ The rugosa species roses are the most resistant to powdery mildew. The Explorer and Parkland series roses are also good choices, but remember, no species is completely immune to powdery mildew.

I have black spots all over my rose leaves. Is this a disease?

Lois ❖ Yes! Blackspot (*Diplocarpon rosae*) is one of the world's most common rose diseases and can kill your plant if left unchecked. Spray all of your roses with fungicide. Remove and discard all diseased foliage, and clear away any fallen leaves. Never put diseased foliage in the compost! Burn it, or seal it in garbage bags.

Jim ❖ Blackspot was first reported in Sweden in 1815. It arrived in the northern US in 1830 and made its way into Canada by 1911. The fungus becomes active when it's immersed in water at 24°C or warmer for at least seven hours. Don't get the leaves wet when you water, and avoid watering late in the evening. Preventive antifungal sprays that contain sulphur and copper mixtures, or chemicals such as maneb, mancozeb and ferbam work well against blackspot.

Emmanuel—double flower, English rose

Flower Carpet—double flower, tender

The undersides of the leaves on my rosebush are covered with orange-red spots. What should I do?

Lois ❖ West Coast gardeners seldom have to worry about cold, but they do have to worry about rose rust. This fungal disease doesn't often occur east of the Rockies.

The best way to avoid rust is to choose rust–resistant varieties. If rust does show up on your plants, remove and destroy any infected leaves. Again, don't put them in your compost.

Jim ❖ Rust thrives in cool, moist weather (18–21°C), particularly when there's rain, mist, or fog. If you live on the West Coast, where damp spells are common, rust can be a serious problem. During damp spells, keep a close watch on those rose plants!

If you do find rust, the best solution is to catch it early and remove all rust pustules. As a preventive measure you could spray mancozeb, ferbam or sulphur (check for availability in your area) to help prevent further spreading. These fungicides do *not* cure the problem—they only prevent healthy growth from becoming infected. You must remove all parts of the plant showing symptoms.

My rose has weird yellow lines and spots on its leaves. What's wrong?

Lois ❖ That's rose mosaic virus. There's no cure for it, but it won't kill your plant, and it won't spread to other roses in your garden. However, that rose bush will never perform up to its potential. If I were you, I'd dig it out and buy a new one.

Jim ❖ This disease is caused by a number of diseases that work together to attack roses. For years, many rosarians believed rose mosaic was relatively benign. They simply trimmed off any branches that showed signs of the disease. We now know, however, that infected plants grow less vigourously, drop their leaves earlier in the fall, and are more likely to be injured by cold.

Rose mosaic is transmitted when a healthy plant is grafted onto infected rootstock, or when cuttings are taken from an infected mother plant. In other words, your rose was diseased when you bought it, even if it showed no symptoms. If you buy your roses only from reputable suppliers, you're much less likely to encounter this disease.

Do any companion plants deter insects?

Jim ❖ Many people believe that companion plants somehow assist the growth of other plants. In fact, the opposite is often true. Many companion plants simply compete for sunlight, water, nutrients, and space.

Marigolds have been known to keep nematodes away. However, nematodes don't pose a threat in areas with cold winters.

Why are the leaves curling on my roses?

Lois ❖ This may be a sign that you're not giving your roses enough water. Aphids also cause the leaves to curl. They leave behind a sticky honeydew, so check your plant and spray if necessary.

Why aren't my rosebuds opening? I can't see any sign of an insect problem.

Jim ❖ This may simply be due to "bullheading"—sometimes the first blooms of the season develop only partially, and then refuse to open. If this is your problem, your plant should bloom normally a little later in the season. Keep an eye on your plant, though. If the symptoms persist, you may have overlooked an insect problem.

Some of my flowers look like little balls. They won't open up properly. What can I do?

Lois ❖ If your bush does this all the time, you might consider digging it out and replacing it with a different variety.

Jim ❖ Some varieties, especially those with lots of petals, experience this problem during humid weather. The petals stick together, and the flower can't unfurl properly. Cut these flowers off, and wait for new and better blooms once the weather gets a bit drier.

My rosebuds are riddled with tiny holes. What's the cause?

Lois ❖ It sounds as if you have rose weevils. They love rosebuds. Remove the rosebuds and destroy them. It's too late to save these flowers, but if you spray with an insecticide like permethrin or rotenone, you'll spare future rosebuds from this sad fate. Whenever you use insecticides, read the instructions carefully.

Jim ❖ The rose curculio (or weevil) is a small, reddish brown beetle that feeds on native roses. With its distinctive long snout, it punches holes into rose buds to lay eggs and feed.

To treat for weevils, remove the damaged rosebuds and spray the plant with permethrin or rotenone before further holes appear. As with most pest problems, your best defense is a healthy plant. Water, fertilize, and keep the area tidy throughout the season.

Some of the canes on my rosebush have strange, round swellings on them. What's wrong, and what should I do about it?

Jim ❖ These swellings, called mossy rose gall, are caused by tiny wasp-like insects (*Diplolepis rosae*). They bore into the canes and lay eggs. As the larvae develop, they secrete chemicals that cause the canes to swell into reddish, moss-like balls about 2–3 cm in diameter. Prune and burn any infected wood.

What is the gnarled lumpy growth at the base of my rose bush?

Jim ❖ This is a bacterial disease called rose gall. At present, there's no cure. You have to dig out that bush and destroy it—don't put it on your compost pile. Also dispose of any soil that has contacted the roots. Afterwards, wash your tools with a bleach solution.

Rose gall, caused by the bacterium *Agrobacterium tumefaciens,* infects a whole assortment of woody shrubs, but roses are a favourite target. The bacteria can remain active in the soil for up to two years. That's why it's important to clean out the whole area around the diseased plant.

spider-mite infestation

My rosebush is losing its leaves. The fallen leaves are dry, stippled, and curled up. Some of them have tiny spiderwebs on them. Why?

Lois ❖ Your bush has been infested with spider mites, one of the most destructive pests that plague roses. They draw the juices out of the underside of leaves. Once they're finished with one leaf, they move on to the next. Left unchecked, they can completely defoliate a rosebush in less than two weeks. Spider mites prefer hot, dry weather, so watch for them during extended warm spells.

Wise Portia—double flower, English rose

Jim ❖ If you keep a close lookout, you might catch a spider-mite problem at an early stage. When you spot any tiny spider webs, give your bush a good spray with your garden hose, paying special attention to the undersides of the leaves. Insecticidal soap helps clear up more severe infestations. Remember that the soap spray must actually contact the bugs, so you need to be thorough. This doesn't kill the eggs, so continue to spray once a week for several weeks to catch any mites that hatch later.

My roses are turning brown and only partially opening. Why?

Jim ❖ It sounds as if you've got thrips. These tiny, needle-like insects feed on many flowers and buds in your garden, including roses. Pull apart and tap your rosebud over a white piece of paper to get a look at these minute pests. To treat your plant, spray with an insecticide such as malathion.

Gruss au Aachen—double flower, floribunda

What's a rose slug?

Jim ❖ They look like greenish, miniature garden slugs—but they aren't slugs! When they show up on your roses (look for them on the undersides of leaves), spray them with insecticide, such as malathion. You can also simply brush them off and squish them, if you're not squeamish. Rose slugs are also referred to as pear slugs.

Rose slugs are actually the larvae of a sawfly, a wasp-like insect. The larvae feed on the undersides of the leaves, skeletonizing them down to nothing but the epidermis, the outermost layer of leaf tissues. Because they're so vulnerable to insecticides, rose slugs don't pose a serious threat. Don't ignore them, though. They can cause a lot of damage if left unchecked.

Some of my roses have a silver film on the leaves— what can it be?

Jim ❖ Slugs have been crawling around in your garden, leaving their telltale slimy trails. Roses aren't particularly prone to slug damage, so don't worry too much unless you have a severe infestation.

If you do have a lot of slugs, Safer's Slug and Snail Bait controls them organically. You can also use any slug bait that has metaldehyde as an active ingredient.

Why do some of my rose leaves have big circles cut out of them?

Lois ❖ Your roses have been visited by leafcutter bees. They only inflict cosmetic damage, so I recommend just putting up with them. When you think of all the benefits bees bring to your garden, it's a small price to pay.

Jim ❖ Unlike honeybees, leafcutter bees don't live in colonies. Instead, individual female bees build brood chambers for their eggs, using those leaf circles as their primary construction material. Since they only cut leaves for a short period early in the season, there's no cause for panic.

How do I get rid of aphids?

Jim ❖ You don't have to worry about killing every single aphid on your rosebush. Rather, you just have to control their numbers. Spray affected plants with insecticidal soap.

You can also try to attract more ladybugs to your garden, since they prey on aphids. You can buy ladybug lures at most garden centres.

The new growth on my roses is red. Why?

Jim ❖ Several things can cause this. Vigourous new shoots naturally tend to be reddish purple. On some varieties, this new growth stays red until chlorophyll develops in the plant.

Cool spring temperatures or a lack of phosphorus and nitrogen can also cause red growth.

aphids

The leaves on my rosebush are turning yellow. What's the cause?

Lois ❖ Your plant's roots may be waterlogged. Any plant starved for oxygen begins to turn yellow. The problem might also be caused by a lack of fertilizer.

Jim ❖ If the lower leaves on your plant were the first to turn yellow, you can be almost certain that your plant is short of nitrogen. If your plant turned yellow evenly, Mom's right—check your soil for proper drainage.

In rare cases a lack of sulphur can turn the whole plant yellow. Iron sulphate alleviates this problem.

What is suckering? Can I prevent it?

Lois ❖ Suckers are the lateral shoots that develop from the roots of a rose. They usually appear when a grafted rose is growing poorly. The rootstock begins sending up its own shoots if the upper grafted growth begins to die. If you do buy grafted roses, plant the crown below the soil level to avoid this problem.

Jim ❖ Some rootstocks tend to produce more suckers than others. Assuming you have completely buried your rootstock, the only thing you can do with suckers is to remove each one as soon as it appears. Follow the shoot down to where it joins the main stem. Cut it off as flush as possible to the main stem—otherwise it may grow back.

How can I get my scraggly rose to become bushier?

Lois ❖ If your rose looks scraggly, you can usually perk it up with a little love and attention. Once again, here's a summary of your rose's basic needs:

- Plenty of sunlight—at least six hours per day.
- Thorough watering, every time the soil begins to dry out.
- Regular fertilizer—20-20-20, 15-15-30, or 28-14-14.
- Pruning—remove any weak or diseased shoots.

My rose won't bloom. Why?

Lois ❖ Your rose probably isn't getting enough light. Sometimes, as our gardens mature, previously sunny locations gradually become shaded. Move your rose to a sunnier location, or consider planting a more shade-tolerant variety.

Jim ❖ If you can't see any obvious signs of disease or insect damage, a light shortage is indeed the likely cause. Your plant may also simply be too young. Roses that bloom only once per season often don't bloom at all during their first season. If you planted your rosebush recently, you might have to wait until next year for flowers.

My climbing rose only flowers at the top of the canes. How can I encourage it to bloom on the lower branches?

Lois ❖ Again, it may be a lack of light. Often, the top part of a climbing rose shades the bottom. Your rose may begin to bloom more evenly if you cut back some of the outside canes to allow more light to reach the lower branches.

Jim ❖ This may also simply be a symptom of age. As canes mature and thicken, they stop producing low growth. If this sounds like your problem, try removing some of the oldest, thickest canes to allow newer growth to fill in.

Mt. Hood—double flower, grandiflora

I purchased a "double" rose, yet it only produces single flowers. What's going on?

Jim ❖ You may simply have been sold the wrong plant. Sometimes plants are given the wrong tags, even before they arrive at a nursery.

If it's a grafted rose, there's also a chance that the top graft has died. When the rootstock takes over and sends out its own shoots, the resulting bush has only the characteristics of the rootstock.

The veins on my rose leaves seem unnaturally prominent. Am I doing something wrong?

Lois ❖ I would guess that your roses aren't getting enough iron.

Jim ❖ When your roses are short of iron, the leaves become very pale, except for the veins. That's why the veins suddenly look so prominent.

This can happen if your soil pH is too high. Iron doesn't dissolve well in alkaline soil. If your soil's pH is too high, your roses won't absorb enough iron, even if you add extra. For roses, the soil pH should be between 6.2 and 6.5.

Test your soil's pH to make sure it falls within that range (purchase a simple test kit at your garden centre). If you discover that pH isn't the problem, add chelated iron to your soil or switch to a rose fertilizer that contains chelated iron. Don't use other forms of iron, such as iron filings—these become 'immobilized' (bound up) in the soil, and as a result aren't available to your plants.

English Garden—double flower, English rose

Gold Medal—double flower, grandiflora

Why do some blooms fade or change colour?

Jim ❖ A number of factors can cause a change in bloom colour:

- Phosphorus deficiency (see fertilizer section).
- Temperature—in general, cool weather intensifies colour while hot weather fades it.
- Age of the flower—blooms appear most vibrant when they first open, and gradually fade as they age.
- Mutation—cells in one bud can mutate, producing a "sport."

What is a "sport"?

Jim ❖ A sport results when a cell or cells mutate (change their genetic make-up). Mutations occur naturally, but can also be induced by breeders. Many mutations produce undesirable shoots and branches, but a few prove highly desirable. Breeders get particularly excited when a bloom colour differs dramatically from that of the mother plant.

Some sports aren't stable (the sport's shoots simply resemble the mother plant), but others continue to produce desirable plants from cuttings. The stability of the sport depends, to a large extent, on the region within the shoot tip where the mutated cells originated.

St. Swithum—double flower, English rose

Will railroad ties treated with creosote hurt my roses?

Jim ❖ If you have a choice, use ties that haven't been treated with creosote. I wouldn't worry, however, provided the ties are well weathered and have no creosote on the surface. Research shows that creosote does not move into the soil to any great degree. I have seen rose leaves damaged by direct contact with a creosote-treated railway tie, but only those leaves were affected.

My roses have been battered by hail. Will they recover?

Lois ❖ Hail damage often looks irreparable, but roses have a remarkable ability to recover. Clean up any fallen petals and foliage, and remove any broken or damaged growth. Give the plants plenty of fertilizer, and they will soon recover.

My dog urinates on my rose bush and it's starting to look unhealthy. What should I do?

Lois ❖ Urine is very high in ammonium salts, which can burn your rosebushes. Water the bush very heavily over the next couple of days to flush away as much of the salt as possible. Then find a way to keep your dog away from that rose!

My hybrid tea roses have long, straight shoots coming up from the base of the plant. They never produce flowers. Why?

Jim ❖ On grafted plants, this happens when the plant above the graft is dead or very weak. The rootstock sends up shoots and suckers. The upper portion of a grafted rose inhibits suckering of the rootstock when it is alive and healthy. If it dies, the rootstock is not inhibited and suckers start to grow. Dig up the plant and replace it with a new one.

The Wife of Bath—double flower, English rose

Lambert Closse—double flower, hardy shrub

My rosebush produces stems that simply stop growing. They don't produce flowers. What's wrong?

Jim ❖ Those are called blind shoots. Some varieties tend to do this more than others. Nobody knows for sure why this happens, but it typically isn't due to disease or insects.

If you do get a blind shoot, cut the stem back to just above the second leaf from the top. This triggers new growth.

There is an anthill in my rose garden. Will ants harm my plants? If so, how can I get rid of them without damaging my plants?

Lois ❖ Ants normally don't pose much of a threat to roses. If an anthill is very close to a stem, the disturbed soil might dry out a little more quickly than normal. Otherwise, if you don't mind ants crawling around the yard, just leave them be.

Jim ❖ When plants perform poorly people often blame ants, but they don't deserve this bad reputation. Keep your roses well watered, and the ants will look for someplace else to build their nests.

If you really need to get rid of the ants, you can choose from a number of insecticides.

Leaves are forming in the centre of my rose blooms. Why?

Jim ❖ Your rose has a condition called phyllody, which causes flower parts to change to leaves. It's most prevalent when roses have been exposed to elevated temperatures or infected with a disease called rose rosette.

What are the other symptoms of rose rosette?

Jim ❖ Rose rosette causes leaves to become distorted and wrinkled. Infected canes send out many short, deformed shoots—this explains the disease's common name, "witch's broom." It is thought to be a viral disease transmitted by mites but this has not been confirmed.

Can I treat for rose rosette?

Jim ❖ If you suspect your rosebush is infected with rose rosette, destroy it immediately and dispose of it. Do not put diseased plants in your compost pile. There's no cure for rose rosette, and it will spread to your other roses.

Fisherman's Friend—double flower, English rose

How can I control weed growth around my thorny rose bushes?

Lois ❖ Here are a few of my favourite methods.

- Always plant into clean soil: eliminate any perennial weeds before planting (i.e., quackgrass, thistle).
- Cover the ground around your roses with mulches like bark, landscape fabrics, etc.
- If all else fails, keep a good stirrup hoe handy—these are effective and easy to use.

Jim ❖ If the weeds are out of control, use Round-Up (glyphosate) around the base of your bush, but be extremely careful not to spray it on the rose itself. Casoron, a soil-applied herbicide, also controls many weeds. Use it with care, though, and only on established plants. Ask the staff at your garden centre for advice on how to apply it.

My roses are growing poorly since I began using well water. Why?

Jim ❖ Have your water tested—you may find out that it's high in sodium. In excessive quantities, sodium deteriorates your soil's structure and as the salts build up in the soil, the roots have a difficult time absorbing water. If your water contains greater than about 70 ppm (parts per million) of sodium, don't use it in your garden. This might be a good time to shop for a rain barrel!

CHAPTER 7 ❧
ROSE VARIETIES

Love miniature roses, but don't like a lot of fragrance? Try Cupcake. A hardy climber with yellow blooms…Alchymist is the best choice. Every rose cultivar has its own advantages and disadvantages, and there are hundreds of worthwhile varieties. Collected here are your questions about your favourite varieties, and the challenges you've faced in their cultivation.

Do climbing roses self-cling?

Jim ❖ The term "climbing rose" is a bit mislead-ing, because unlike many vines (such as Virginia creeper and sweet peas), roses do not produce tendrils. You must train roses and attach their branches to the support.

Although roses sometimes naturally weave through lattice structures, it's a good idea to steer them along. To train a climbing rose, gently push the tip through the lattice as it grows or if necessary, tie it loosely to the trellis. Use soft material, such as foam-covered wire, string or cloth, to avoid damaging the stems.

Some Climbing Roses

Alchymist
Captain Samuel Holland
Frühlingsgold
Frühlingsmorgen
Henry Kelsey
John Cabot
John Davis
Louis Jolliet
Max Graf
Quadra
The Polar Star
William Baffin

What types of support do you recommend for climbing roses?

Lois ❖ Any well anchored, strong, fairly "open" trellis provides good support. Don't use a tightly woven lattice, however, because rose canes get thick quite rapidly.

William Baffin and John Cabot—Explorer roses

Stanwell Perpetual—double flower, old garden rose

Which varieties of roses attract butterflies?

Lois ❖ I'm afraid butterflies don't share our passion for roses. Your rosebushes might attract plenty of admirers, but you won't find butterflies among them.

Jim ❖ Butterflies search for nectar, and roses don't produce it! Roses in the wild usually self-pollinate (with the exception of pollen spread by wind, rain, or the occasional insect). Since they don't require insects for pollination, roses don't produce nectar.

Who developed English Roses?

Lois ❖ David Austin, the son of an English farmer (and a farmer himself) introduced the first English rose in 1969. After years of effort, he managed to combine the fragrance and delicate hues of old garden roses with the sturdiness and re-blooming characteristics of modern roses.

Austin currently grows millions of roses every year at his nursery in Albrighton, Wolverhampton, England. He has personally introduced about 100 cultivars—truly a great rosarian!

Some English Roses

Abraham Darby
Charles Austin
Charles Rennie Mackintosh
English Garden
Evelyn
Fair Bianca
Fisherman's Friend
Gertrude Jekyll
Glamis Castle
Graham Thomas
Heritage
L.D. Braithwaite
Lilian Austin
Mary Rose
Peach Blossom
Redouté
St. Swithun
The Alexandra Rose
The Countryman
The Pilgrim

Abraham Darby—double flower, English rose

Blue Nile—double flower, hybrid tea

Why can't I find a true blue rose?

Lois ❖ Blue roses are the Holy Grail of rose gardening! Countless growers have tried to produce blue roses, but nobody has succeeded. Some roses have lavender hues, however, such as Blue Nile or Blueberry Hill. Given recent advances in plant breeding and biotechnology, I predict that it won't be long before breeders succeed in their quest to produce a true blue rose.

Jim ❖ Horticulturists are fascinated by the challenge of bringing new colours to traditional flowers. Blue roses would be impossible through traditional plant breeding, because the genes for blue pigmentation simply don't exist in roses.

Genetic engineering, on the other hand, is not about breeding—it's about inserting genetic material from one organism to another. As a result, we may see not only blue roses in the future, but a multitude of other unusual colours as well.

Chicago Peace—double flower, hybrid tea

Are there any black roses?

Jim ❖ Not yet. As with the blue rose, however, I'm sure it's just a matter of time.

A few varieties come very close. The Black Jade miniature rose produces black buds that open into very dark red flowers. Superb Tuscan, an Old Garden Rose, also produces dark-red, almost black flowers, as does the variety Night Time, a hybrid tea.

Likewise, the Mister Lincoln hybrid tea rose isn't truly black, but it does have one of the darkest red hues of all roses. It also has a very prominent "damask" fragrance.

I want to be able to cut long-stemmed roses. Which varieties should I grow?

Lois ❖ Choose hybrid teas if you want traditional long-stemmed flowers similar to those you'd find at a florist's. Most garden roses produce small clusters of flowers on shorter stems.

Lilian Austin—double flower, English rose

Are any rose bushes grown for their foliage?

Some Roses for Fall Colour

Blanc Double de Coubert
Charles Albanel
Dart's Dash
Fimbriata
Frau Dagmar Hartopp
Hansa
Jens Munk
Pavement Roses
Red Frau Dagmar Hartopp
Red Rugosa
Scabrosa
Schneezwerg
Thèrése Bugnet
White Rugosa

Lois ❖ The most striking variety is the Wingthorn rose. It produces large, spectacular translucent red thorns. The Red-leaf rose, with its reddish purple foliage, is another standout. Other varieties are prized for their vibrant fall leaf colours or showy rosehips.

Jim ❖ Another unusual variety is the Sweetbriar rose, known for its fragrant foliage. Sweetbriar leaves have a wonderful fragrance, particularly after a rain.

Are there any green-flowered roses?

Jim ❖ The unique St. Patrick, a hybrid tea, is the one variety that comes close. It produces apple-green rosebuds that bloom into a beautiful lemon-yellow tinged with green. Warm temperatures tend to bring out more of the green shade, while cooler temperatures enhance the vibrancy of the yellow tones. Whatever the weather, though, this is a very striking rose!

Thèrése Bugnet—double flower, hardy shrub

St. Patrick—double flower, hybrid tea

What is the hardiest climbing rose?

Lois ❖ I recommend the sturdy Polar Star. This hardy shrub has an extremely vigorous growth habit, producing dazzling white flowers. The Explorer series also includes many outstanding choices. My favourites are John Cabot and William Baffin.

Are there any rose varieties that don't produce thorns?

Lois ❖ J.P. Connell and Rita Bugnet have few or no thorns.

Jim ❖ All roses are thornless!

We couldn't write a whole book on roses without mentioning this bit of trivia. Those pointed things on rose stems are actually not thorns or spines—they're prickles. Strictly speaking, a thorn is a modified stem, and a spine is a modified leaf. A prickle, on the other hand, is an outgrowth of the epidermis.

True, it may be a minor point, but you have to be sharp in this business!

Will tender climbing roses survive harsh winters?

Lois ❖ Yes, but you must lay them down on the ground in the fall and protect them with plenty of mulch. I recommend generous layers of peat moss and newspaper, topped off with a nice big pile of snow.

Jim ❖ Protecting tender climbing roses is a painstaking process, but you must if you want them to survive a cold winter.

1. Inspect the plant carefully, and prune out any dead or diseased branches.

2. Carefully take the plant down from the trellis, and bury it in the ground. Or take the plant down, trellis and all.

3. Add a generous layer of mulch (I prefer peat moss).

4. Cover the mulch with a plastic sheet, securely anchored, and a final light layer of soil. When it snows, throw a few shovels full onto the pile.

Some Groundcover Roses

Charles Albanel
Dart's Dash
Double White Burnet
Frau Dagmar Hartopp
Max Graf
Nozomi
Pavement Roses
Red Frau Dagmar Hartopp

Is there a difference between a rambler rose and a groundcover rose?

Jim ❖ Not really. At our greenhouse we classify them in the same category: landscape roses. The only difference is that rambler roses are specifically derived from the species *Rosa wichuriana,* whereas groundcover roses come from many species. Ramblers form thick, dense shrubs, and are often planted in mass for effect.

Another technical difference is that the branches of ramblers will not produce roots easily, whereas groundcover rose canes often set root and sprout wherever they touch the ground. As a result, they spread.

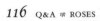

Which species is the Alberta wild rose? Can I purchase it?

Lois ❖ Alberta claims the "prickly rose" as its provincial flower, but it grows across most of the country, from British Columbia to Quebec. The flowers are a lovely soft pink with large yellow stamens. It is available at some specialty garden centres.

Jim ❖ The Alberta wild rose (*Rosa acicularis*) is the largest and most widespread wild rose in Canada. It's one of our most striking native plants, producing large 5–8-cm blooms from June to July. Wild roses prefer moist soil, which is why you find so many growing in ditches and along roadsides.

The wild roses I see in southern Alberta look different than those farther north. Are they different species?

Lois ❖ A single variety of rose, grown in two different climates, may end up looking like two separate species! Wild roses prefer cool, moist conditions. Knowing how hot and dry it can be in southern Alberta, I'm not surprised the roses looks different.

Jim ❖ Mom's right—it probably boils down to a difference in climate. However, the two roses may also be different species. Alberta has five native species of wild rose: the familiar *Rosa acicularis*, the closely related but less common *Rosa woodsii* ("Wood's rose"), *Rosa arkansana, Rosa arkansana* var. *suffulta,* and *Rosa macounii.*

Alberta Native Rose Species

Rosa acicularis
• most familiar wild rose in Alberta

Rosa arkansana
• blooms for 2-3 weeks in June/July

Rosa arkansana var. suffulta
• blooms recurrently for 3-5 weeks in July/August

Rosa macounii
• blooms recurrently for 3-5 weeks in July/August

Rosa woodsii
• blooms for 4-5 weeks in May/June
• virtually identical to *macounii,* but with much smaller leaves

My friend's floribunda rose has beautiful, evenly rounded masses of blossoms. On mine, though, some of the blossoms are much bigger than others. How can I make my rosebush look like hers?

Lois ❖ I like the natural look of floribundas— one large rose on each stem, surrounded by many other smaller ones. To get the rounded, even look you describe, however, you have to pinch the buds. Simply pinch out the fat, centre bud, and the surrounding buds will have more room to develop.

Jim ❖ You might also have different varieties. Floribundas can vary greatly in bloom size.

My flower carpet rose is growing laterally! What can I do about it?

Lois ❖ Groundcover roses are low spreading roses and naturally incline towards the ground. Hence the name "carpet."

Is rose of Sharon a rose?

Lois ❖ No, it's not a rose at all. It's a tender perennial, a member of the mallow family (*Hibiscus syriacus*), and produces white, pink or purplish hibiscus-like flowers.

What kind of rose is the rose tree of China?

Lois ❖ Again, this is not a rose. It is also known as double-flowering plum. It produces plentiful flowers that resemble tiny Hansa roses.

Some Hybrid Tea Roses

Dainty Bess
Double Delight
Electron
Elina
Elizabeth Taylor
First Prize
Folklore
Fragrant Cloud
Garden Party
Granada
Miss All-American Beauty
Mister Lincoln
Olympiad
Painted Moon
Paradise
Pascali
Paul Shirville
Peace
Pristine
Royal Highness
St. Patrick
Secret
Tiffany
Touch of Class

Is there a substitute for alchymist rose?

Lois ❖ It's hard to suggest a substitute for this hardy yellow climbing rose. It sells out almost every spring, however, so we hear that question a lot. Frülingsgold (also known as Spring Morning) is a good substitute. It is another hardy yellow climber and has lovely, fragrant blossoms.

What's the best Explorer rose?

Jim ❖ All of the climbing Explorer roses are very popular. Among my favourites are William Baffin, John Cabot, and Henry Kelsey.

What can I substitute for Hansa rose?

Jim ❖ If you can't find a Hansa rose, consider one of the Rugosa varieties. Rugosas are extremely hardy and make excellent, showy hedges. Thèrése Bugnet is another good substitute.

What are "Pavement roses"?

Lois ❖ These roses got their name because of their growth habit. They're perfect for growing along sidewalks and driveways. They grow well even in poor soil and tolerate the sidewalk salt left over from the winter. Best of all, they produce beautiful blooms all summer long.

Jim ❖ This is one tough rose! It tolerates extreme cold and also stands up to heat and drought. If people tell me that they tend to kill off their roses, I recommend this almost indestructible rose series.

Snow Pavement—double flower, hardy shrub

What are Parkland roses?

Parkland Roses

Adelaide Hoodless
Cuthbert Grant
Morden Amorette
Morden Blush
Morden Cardinette
Morden Centennial
Morden Fireglow
Morden Ruby
Morden Sunrise
Morden Snow Beauty
Winnipeg Parks

Lois ❖ This wonderful series of roses was developed at Agriculture Canada's research station in Morden, Manitoba. In the 1960s, they began to breed roses specifically for the northern prairies, with their frigid winters and hot, dry summers. In 1967, Morden Station introduced the first Parkland rose, Cuthbert Grant, with instant success. They have continued their work over the decades. There are many different Parkland roses available.

Parkland roses grow on their own roots, have excellent resistance to disease, and are hardy to zone 2, provided they have adequate snow cover. In other words, they can withstand winter temperatures of -40°C. They produce abundant blossoms on small to medium rosebushes.

Jim ❖ The scientists at Morden had the brilliant idea of crossing the native prairie rose (*Rosa arkansana*) with floribunda and hybrid tea roses. They managed to combine the hardiness of the prairie rose with some of the showy characteristics of its more tender cousins.

Morden Fireglow—double flower, hardy shrub

Henry Kelsey—double flower, hardy shrub, climber

What are Explorer roses?

Lois ❖ These hardy roses are mostly named for Canada's early explorers. Like their namesakes, they successfully braved Canada's harsh climate.

Today, people can choose from more than two dozen Explorer Series roses. All of them offer spectacular blooming, excellent disease resistance and winter hardiness down to zones 2 and 3 (with adequate snow cover).

Jim ❖ Again, we can thank Agriculture Canada for this remarkable series. It has been called the most successful series of hardy roses ever introduced, and it certainly lives up to that reputation at our greenhouse. Year after year, the Explorers are our top-selling hardy roses.

Unfortunately, funding for this amazingly successful program has been cut. This is a real pity, considering that the Explorer series has made an international impact, providing Canada with unprecedented rose exports.

Explorer Roses

Alexander Mackenzie
Captain Samuel Holland
Champlain
Charles Albanel
David Thompson
Frontenac
George Vancouver
Henry Hudson
Henry Kelsey
J.P. Connell
Jens Munk
John Cabot
John Davis
John Franklin
Louis Jolliet
Martin Frobisher
Simon Fraser
William Baffin

What is a hybrid musk rose?

Jim ❖ They are a diverse class developed by Reverend Joseph Pemberton in the early twentieth Century. They are characterized by their beauty, vigour, and stong fragrance.

My J.P. Connell Rose had yellow flowers on it when I bought it and this year they all seem to be white. Why is this?

Jim ❖ J.P. Connell tends to produce yellow flowers during cool weather, and white flowers during warmer weather. Often, individual flowers even change colour—growing from deep butter-yellow buds into creamy or bright-white blossoms. I've even seen both colours on the same plant at the same time!

J.P. Connell—double flower, hardy shrub

Afterword
by Jim Hole

I love to learn. I guess that's why I've always been more interested in the mechanics of the real world than the imaginary narratives of novels or films. Don't get me wrong—I love a good story as much as the next guy, but a chance to learn about the inner workings of nature holds more appeal for me. Sometimes Mom describes me as a kind of walking gardening encyclopaedia, but the truth is, as you might have guessed, a little more complex. Although my sister-in-law calls me "Mr. Science," I don't pretend to know everything. But it bugs me if someone asks me a question and I don't know the answer. More often than not, the solution isn't in my head; I have to pull out a textbook or consult a specialist. Over the years I've naturally assimilated plenty of gardening knowledge because of that inability to let a question go without a response. Putting together these books has been very fulfilling for that reason; your questions gave me plenty of opportunity to do some extra research and discover a number of things I wasn't previously aware of.

But there are some questions science can't answer. Sometimes we have to look to aesthetics and history to explain our fascination with certain plants. This is certainly the case with roses. One could ask why they aren't simply lumped in with shrubs. After all, that's all roses are. But there's something about a rose that captures the imagination of painters and playwrights, sculptors and singers. Personally, it's the unique varieties that stop me in my tracks—like the incredibly fragrant Scentimental or the Wingthorn, with its showy spines. Sure, there's an evolutionary reason for these roses to have these characteristics...but sometimes, it's enough to just stop and—well—smell them.

So Ask Us Some Questions...

We plan to update all of the Question and Answer books periodically. If you have a gardening question that's been troubling you, write to us! While we *can't* answer your inquiries individually, your question may appear in future Q&A books—along with the answer, naturally. And don't ever think that a question is "dumb" or "too simple." Odds are that any mysteries you face are shared by countless other gardeners.

Send your questions to:
Hole's Q&A Questions
101 Bellerose Drive
St. Albert, AB T8N 8N8
CANADA

You can also email us at: yourquestions@enjoygardening.com
or visit us at www.enjoygardening.com

Index

Question: *Who is Lois Hole?*

Answer ❖ The author of eight best-selling books, Lois Hole provides practical advice that's both accessible and essential. Her knowledge springs from years of hands-on experience as a gardener and greenhouse operator. She's shared that knowledge for years through her books, her popular newspaper columns, hundreds of gardening talks all over the continent, and dozens of radio and television appearances. Never afraid to get her hands dirty, Lois answers all of your gardening questions with warmth and wit.

Question: *Who is Jim Hole?*

Answer ❖ Inheriting his mother's love of horticulture, Jim Hole grew up in the garden. After spending his formative years on the Hole farm in St. Albert, Jim attended the University of Alberta, expanding his knowledge and earning a Bachelor of Science in Agriculture. Jim appears regularly on radio and television call-in shows to share what he's learned, and writes a weekly gardening column for the *Edmonton Journal*. Jim's focus is on the science behind the garden—he explains what makes plants tick with a clear and concise style, without losing sight of the beauty and wonder that makes gardening worthwhile.

Lois and Jim have worked together for years on books, newspaper articles, and gardening talks. Working with family members Ted Hole, Bill Hole, and Valerie Hole, Lois and Jim helped to create Hole's, a greenhouse and garden centre that ranks among the largest retail gardening operations in Canada. The books in the *Q&A* series mark Lois and Jim's first official collaboration.

"One last question..."

How did a Q&A book about roses come about?

When the time came to decide on a subject for the second volume in the *Q&A* series, roses were the obvious choice. Given the relatively short time we've been growing roses professionally, these beautiful plants have led to an amazing number of questions.

To collect the questions and provide the answers, we first went to our staff. Our greenhouse and nursery staff collected all the questions they had on file and began searching their memories for others. **Liz Grieve** did a rough sort and separated the rose questions from all the rest. Then **Bill Hole, Jim Hole, Valerie Hole**, and **Bruce Keith** sorted through the questions, identified the weak spots, and set to work finding new questions to fill in the gaps.

As was the case for the first *Q&A* volume, *Bedding Plants*, Jim Hole sat down with **Julia Mamolo** to complete the first rough answers. These were passed on to **Lois & Ted Hole** for their perspective and then on to the rest of the family for the first kick at refinement. Meanwhile, Jim hit the books and quizzed colleagues to dig for the facts.

As the rough text began to emerge **Scott Rollans**, the series editor, began to shape and define the material into book form. Working with the text, he beat the rough material into its final form. As the information poured in and the answers were refined, the text was passed back and forth between the staff to polish and hone into the final manuscript. Meanwhile **Earl Woods** began to write the introductions and collect extra material for the book.

The text then went back to Jim and our resident rose experts, **Shane Neufeld** and **Stephen Raven**, to make sure we had the latest information and final decisions on any differences of opinion. Concurrently the text hit the production department, and pictures and charts were organized by designer **Greg Brown** as he began work on the layout and design.

When all the pieces were in place the experts made a final check for accuracy and Bruce, Scott and Earl proofed the pages, preparing it for the finishing design touches. Finally the book was turned over to **Leslie Vermeer** for one final complete proof before it was sent off to the printer.

Publication Direction ❖ Bruce Timothy Keith
Series Editor ❖ Scott Rollans
Editorial Assistant ❖ Julia Mamolo
Proofing ❖ Leslie Vermeer
Additional Writing & Editing ❖ Earl J. Woods
Book Design and Production ❖ Gregory Brown